Carving From Roughouts With Tom Wolfe

Tom Wolfe

Schiffer Publishing Ltd®

4880 Lower Valley Road, Atglen, PA 19310 USA

Library of Congress Catalog Card Number:98-89211

This book is meant only for personal home use and recreation. It is not intended for commercial applications or manufacturing purposes.

Book Designed by Randy L. Hensley
Type set in Windsor BT/Souvenir Lt Bt

ISBN: 0-7643-0736-3

Printed in China

Published by Schiffer Publishing Ltd.
4880 Lower Valley Road
Atglen, PA 19310
Phone: (610) 593-1777; Fax: (610) 593-2002
E-mail: Schifferbk@aol.com
Please visit our web site catalog at **www.schifferbooks.com**

This book may be purchased from the publisher.
Include $3.95 for shipping.
Please try your bookstore first.
We are interested in hearing from authors
with book ideas on related subjects.
You may write for a free catalog.

In Europe, Schiffer books are distributed by
Bushwood Books
6 Marksbury Rd.
Kew Gardens
Surrey TW9 4JF England
Phone: 44 (0)181 392-8585; Fax: 44 (0)181 392-9876
E-mail: Bushwd@aol.com

Introduction

Fishing is one of those things that always starts out the same way, but you never know if you'll end up with a keeper, a catfish, or a story. Sometimes you just end up, like our fisherman here. Carving with roughouts is a lot like fishing.

A roughout is the start of a carving that skips the first few steps to take you right into the "good part". Using a duplicator, you can make several at a time. Many carvers, including me, have their own style of roughout that suits their needs; they also make good teaching tools.

At first it might seem that these "blank" figures would restrict you to the same kind of carving again and again. Actually, roughouts are great for developing your creative eye, because they have a basic but distinct shape that lets your imagination take off. You can make all kinds of different carvings with the same starting point, and you'll be amazed at the many directions they take. The rough figure might have its own shape, but no one said which side was the front, back, top, or bottom. That's up to you to decide. Hold the roughout one way and maybe you've got a grizzly old rebel in the making; turn it upside down and there's a lazy bullfrog.

This book is a step-by-step guide to carving a trout fisherman, if that's all you want it to be. The steps are particularly in-depth though the carving of the face, hands, clothing. and other features. To get the most out of this excercise, though, think most about the *journey* instead of the destination. It's really a lesson in staying loose with the figure. Give it the freedom to become what it wants to be—a keeper, a catfish, or a story. You'll notice that I change my mind while I'm carving time and time again as I see different possibilities come out in the wood. Don't look too far ahead, you might miss something!

Contents

The Roughout

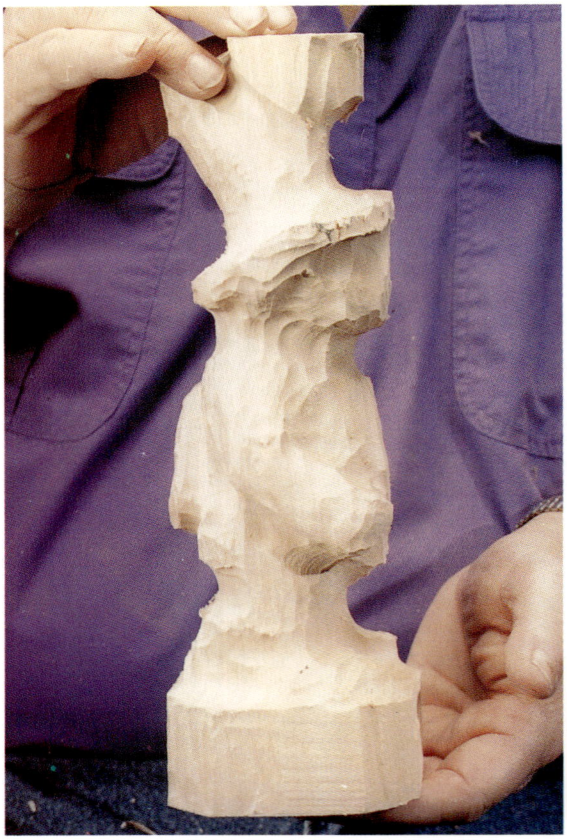

The roughout was done on a duplicater. I have included the pattern for your use, but the real purpose of this book is to show the kinds of variations you can get from a single roughout, no matter which one you choose. This particular one is available from me.

The Carving Process

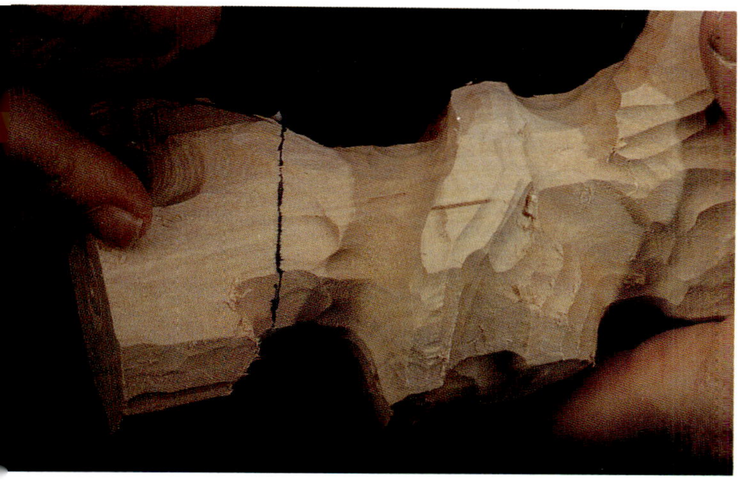

I'm going to mark the crown of the hat.

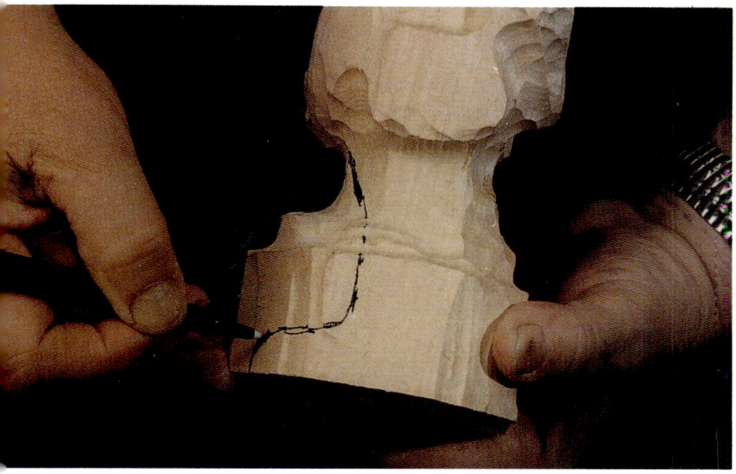

The leg is elongated into the base. Draw the leg and the foot.

Draw the back of the leg. I should mention that for this book I am using a black pen so the camera picks it up; it's better to use a pencil.

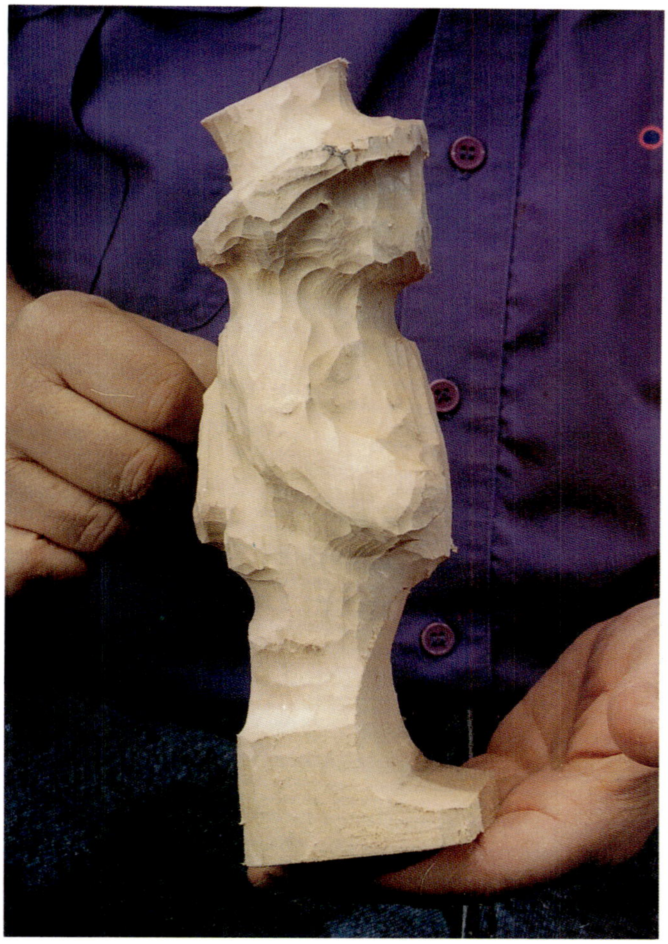

Saw off the excess for this result.

When Harold Enlow saw the cut-off piece from the top of the head he said "Waste not, want not" and carved this bowl-back camel yakicorn.

Use your finger to measure from each side, and mark between them for the center.

Mark a bow between the legs.

Saw the bow for this result.

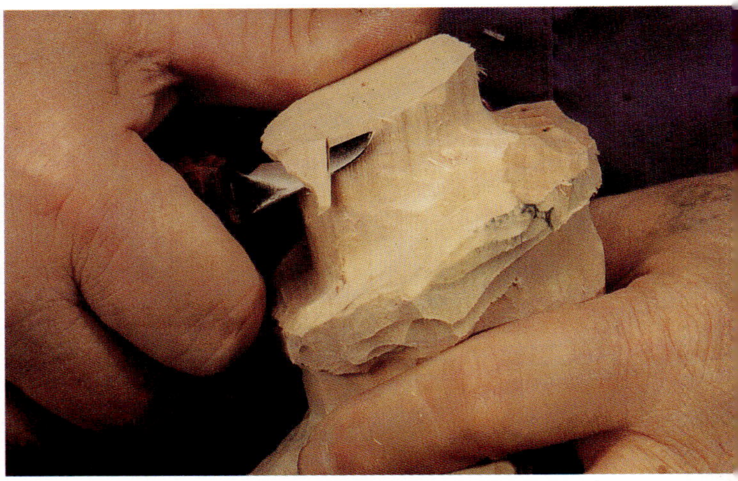

The thickness of the crown of the hat determines the width of the face. I want to narrow the crown of this hat. The length is okay.

I want the crown to be oval when viewed from the top.

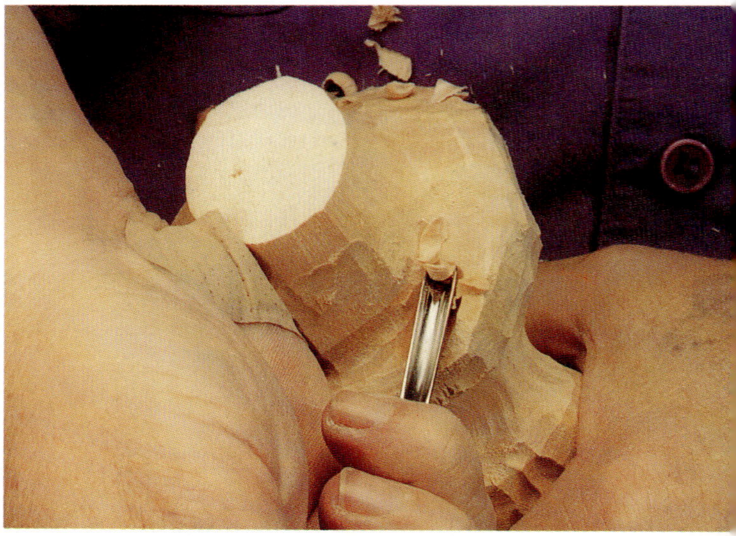

Next we shape the brim. It is better to come from the back because of the direction of the grain. You could use a rotary tool with a round ball bit to do this job. I'm using a gouge.

Continue all the way around.

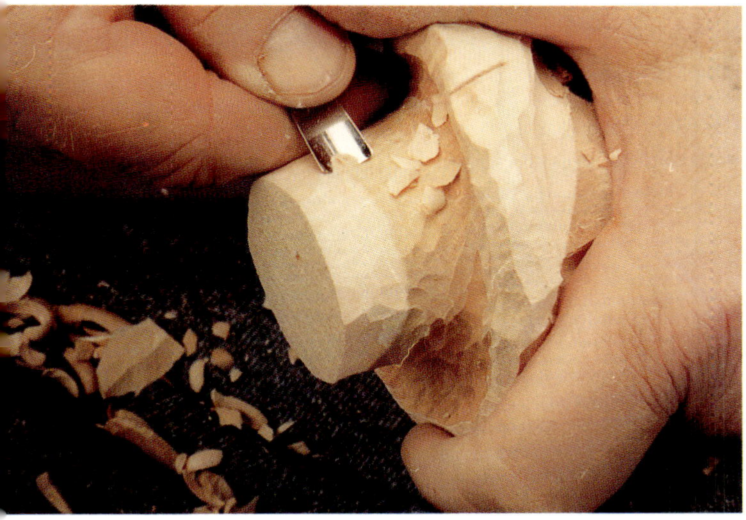

I'm blending the brim into the crown of the hat, still working from the back on up to stay with the grain.

I'm rounding off the edge of the crown to eliminate saw marks.

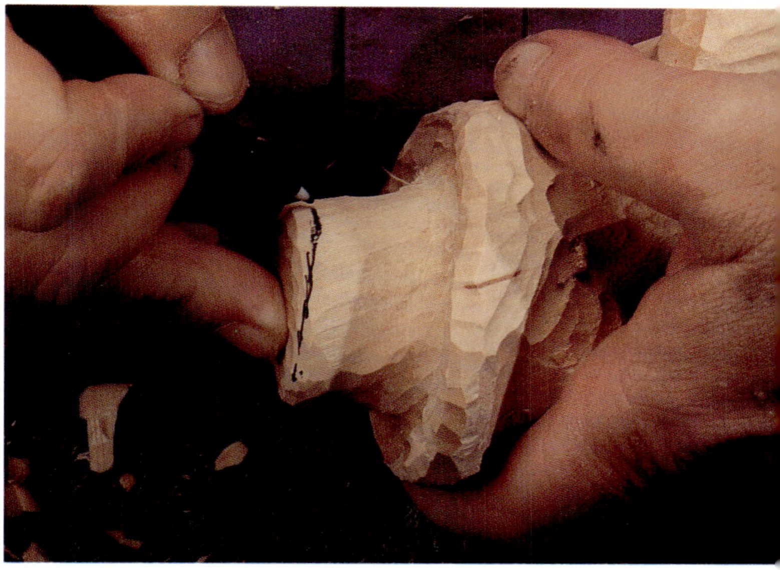

The slope of the crown does not match the slope of the brim, so I'm leveling it off.

Progress on the hat.

Now you can start to see where the face will be in proportion to that hat.

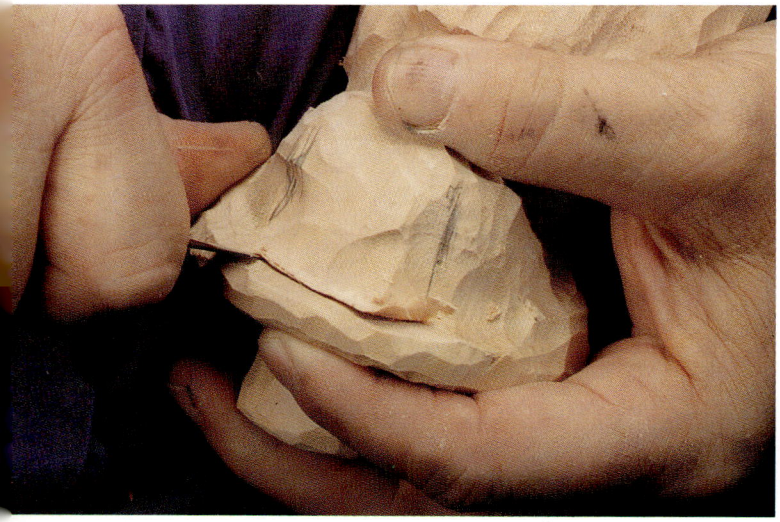

I'm making a stop cut in the front of the brim.

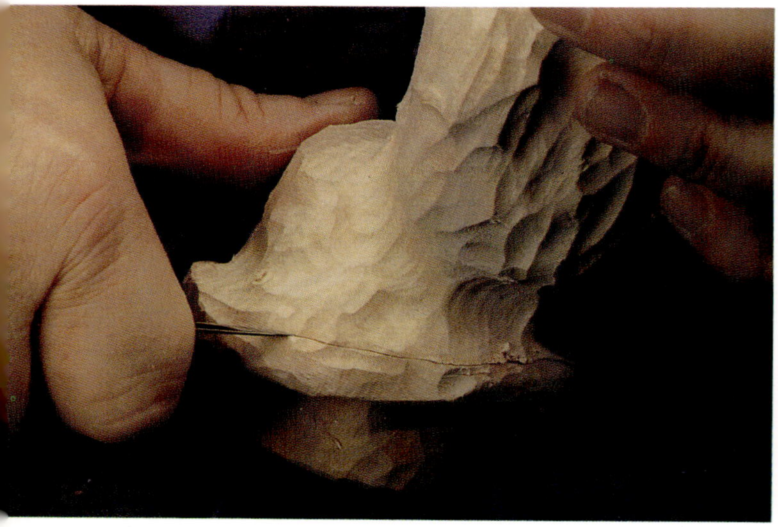

Make the cut all the way around, but leave more thickness on each side for hair and sideburns.

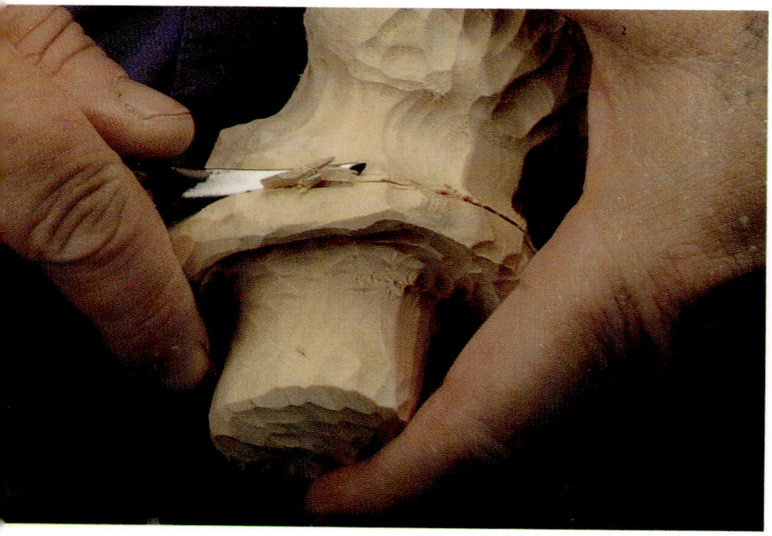

I'm working all the way around in an upward direction.

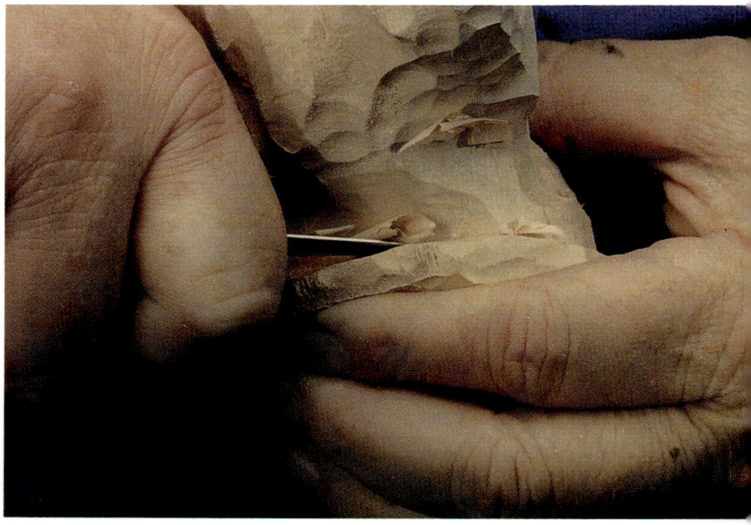

It helps to keep a finger on top of the brim to keep you from cutting in too deeply from underneath. Try it, it works!

Don't cut as much out of the back of the head as in front—leave room for the hair.

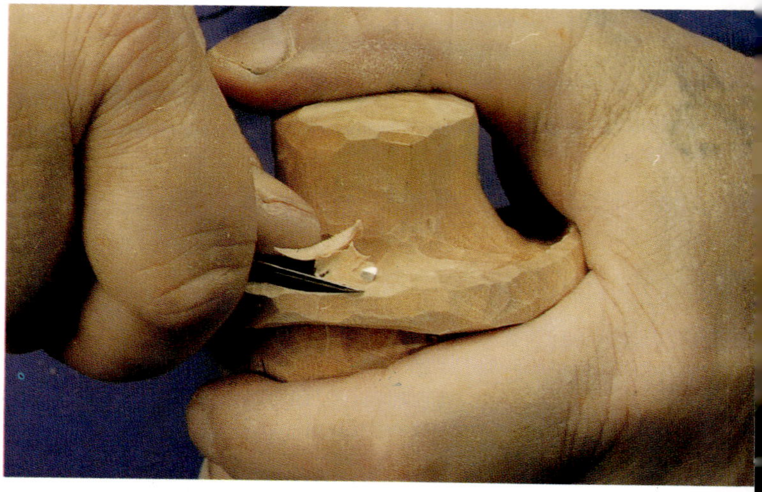

Add a little dip to the front and back of the brim for a more natural look.

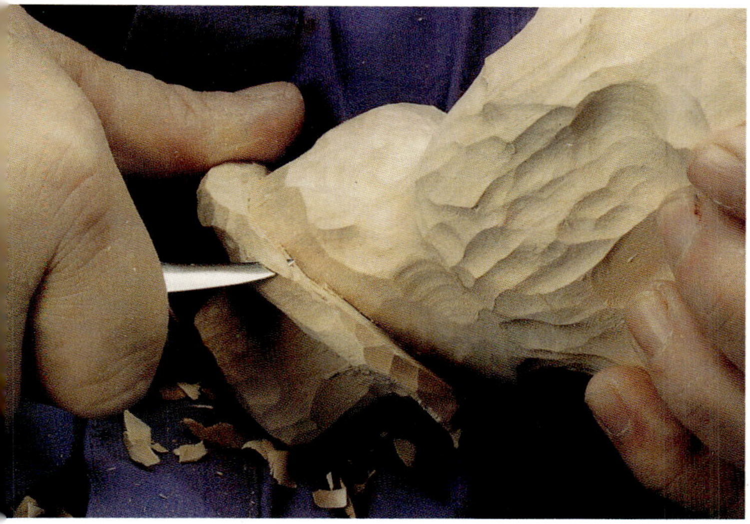

Round the edges to roll the brim up on the sides.

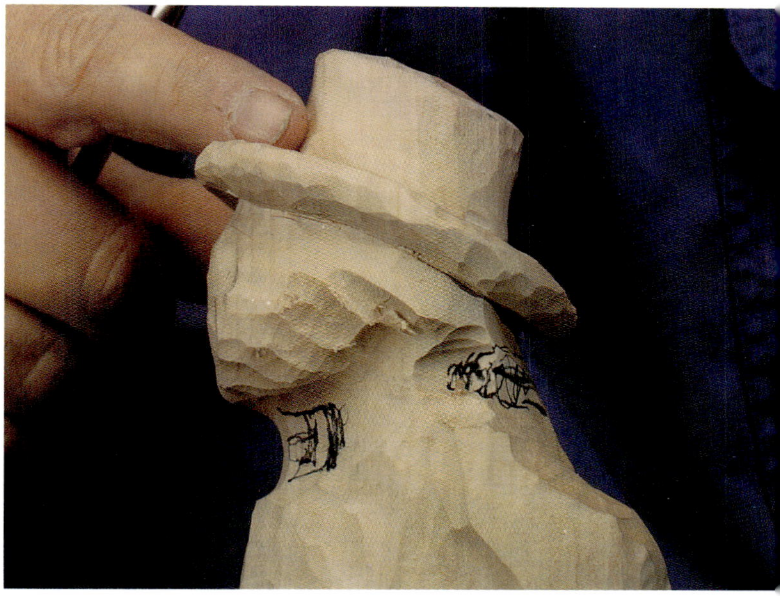

Now I'll begin work on the neck. I prefer a thinner neck, so I have a good bit to cut away.

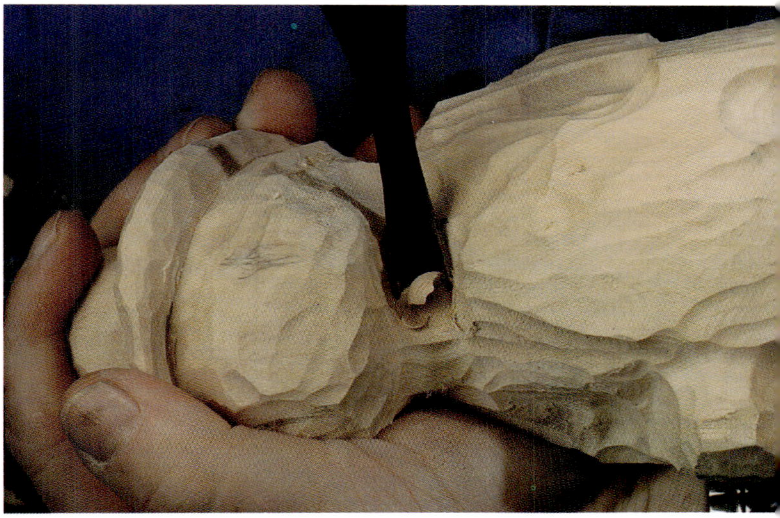

I've started in the front.

Progress.

Progress. I've started with a gouge, and I'll finish with a knife to get a cleaner look.

The knife makes a cleaner cut.

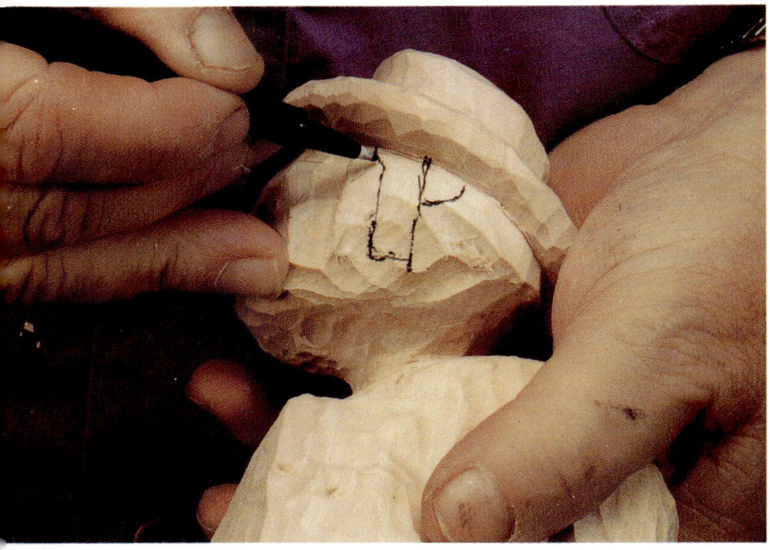

To figure out the position of the ear and hair, make a halfway mark on the head. This line defines the front of the ear, the back of the sideburns, and the top of the jawbone.

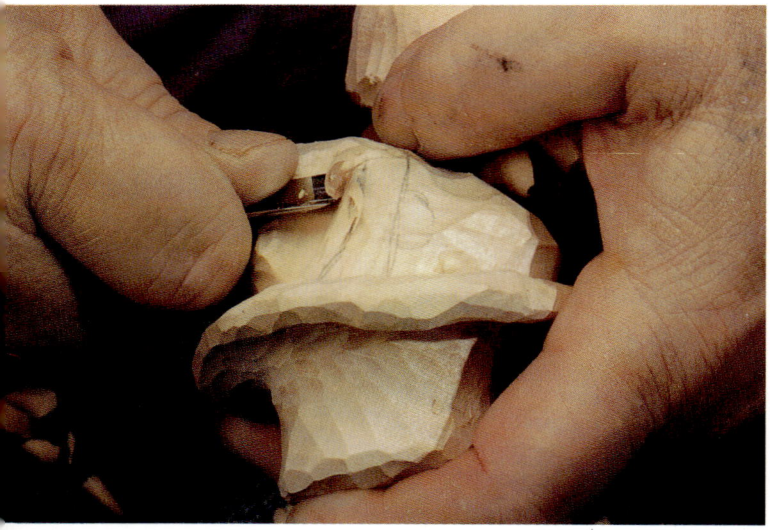

Working from the front of the face, I'm bringing out the side-burns. No need to cut a stop here; we're working with the grain and with a little twist the pieces should pop right off.

Progress. I'm looking over the head to make sure all the lumps are in the right place.

I've noticed that the hat sits differently over each ear. I'm going to take advantage of that and lower the brim itself so the hat looks cocked to one side. I'll take more out of the inside of the brim...

...then a bit off the edge.

I always do the hat first. It really decides the figure's personality, as much as the nose or eyes.

Progress.

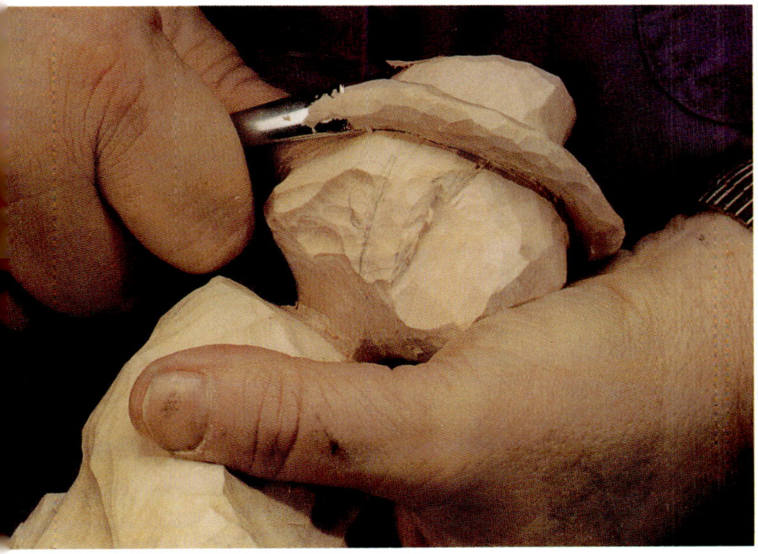

I think I'll bring up the other side for more of an angle.

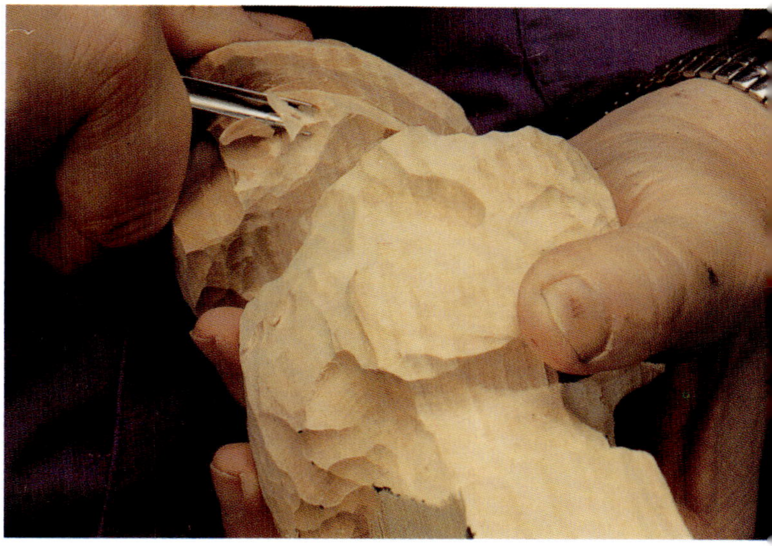

I think our fisherman spends more time fishing than he would in a barber shop, so we'll leave the hair long all the way around. I'm using a half-round gouge to get our hairline.

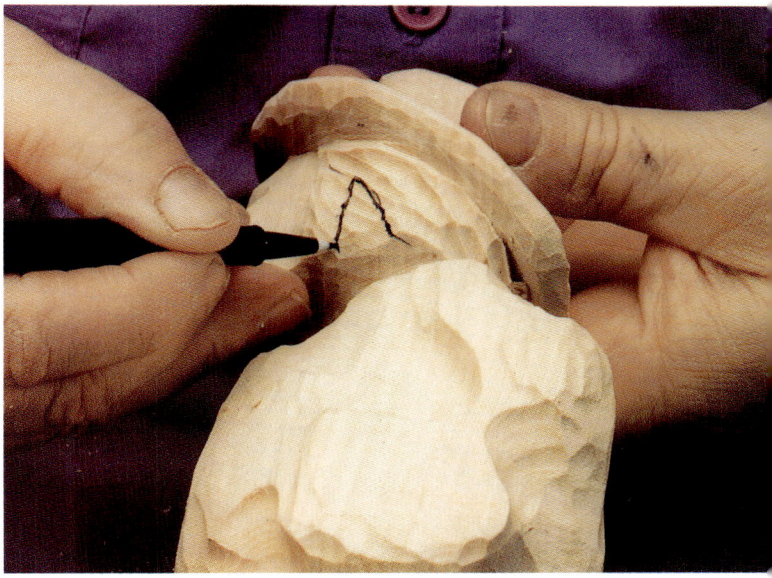

I won't carve the ear until I'm ready to do the nose, but I still need to mark a place for it between the sideburn and the hairline.

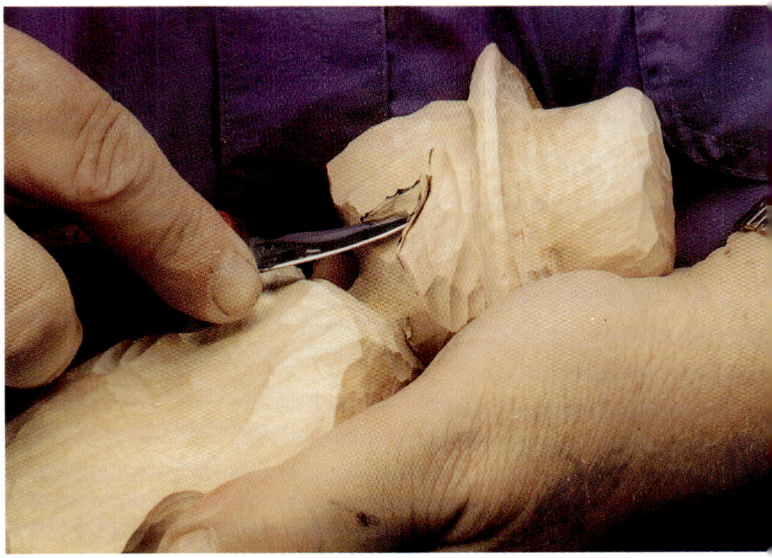

I use a knife that bends a little; it's very helpful in notches like this.

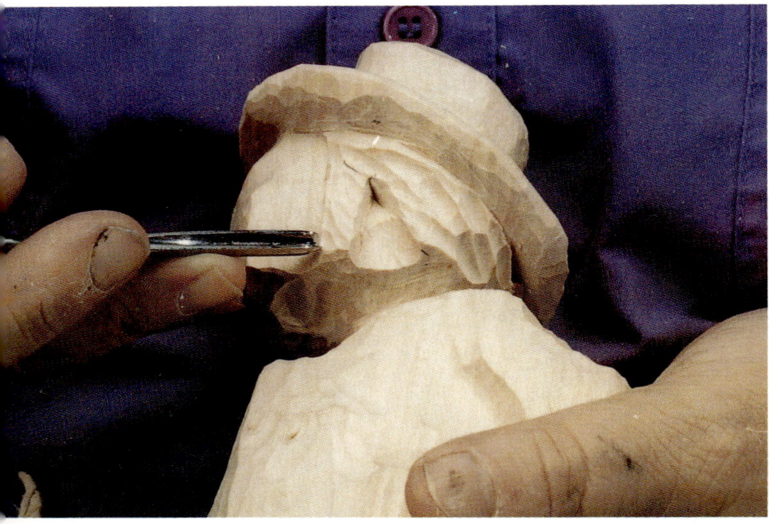

Progress. Remember that the sideburns can be as long as you'd like them.

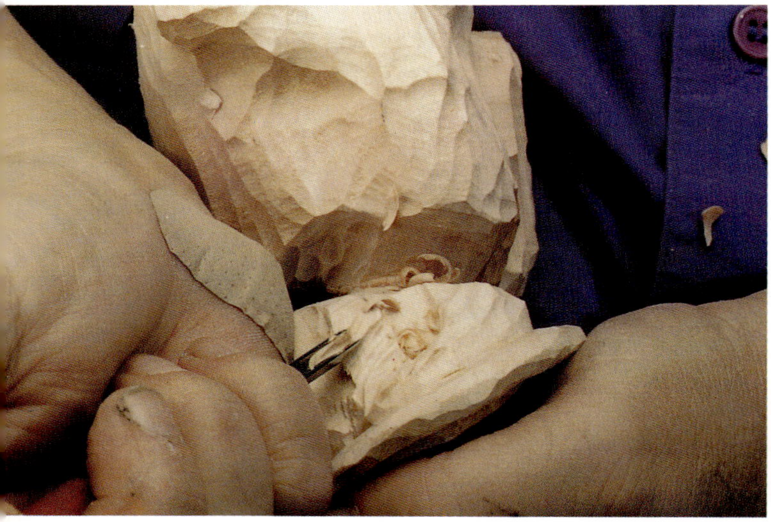

I've decided I want the sideburns closer to the face, and the hair can bush out behind them.

Progress.

Now I am defining the face, beginning with nose. Remember, even though you need to have a good grip on the figure, be careful not to squeeze the hat too much, it's been carved pretty thin!

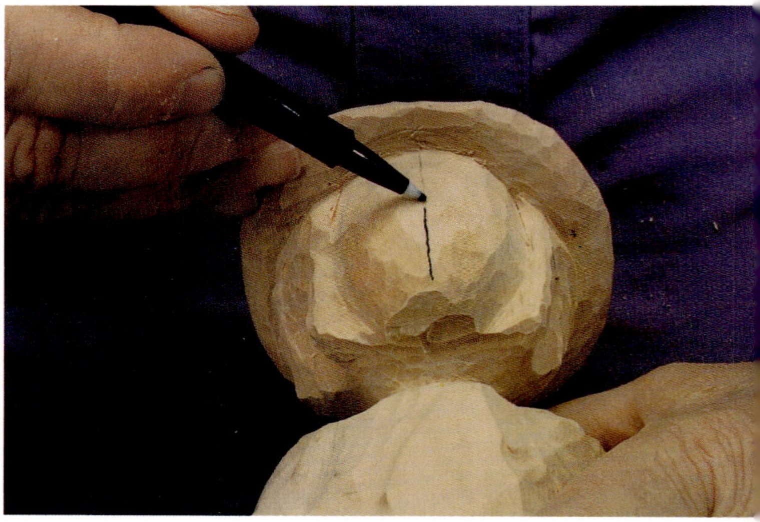

The face starts with a center line. Now is the time to fix any mistakes; here the forehead is too big on one side so I'll round that off.

Once the vertical line is established, I draw a horizontal one where the eyes go. Midway between the eye-line and the chin, place one for the bottom of the nose, and then one dividing what's left in half for the mouth line.

The object here is to pull the face back while leaving the nose as full as possible. I'm starting around the eyes, leaving the bridge of the nose intact.

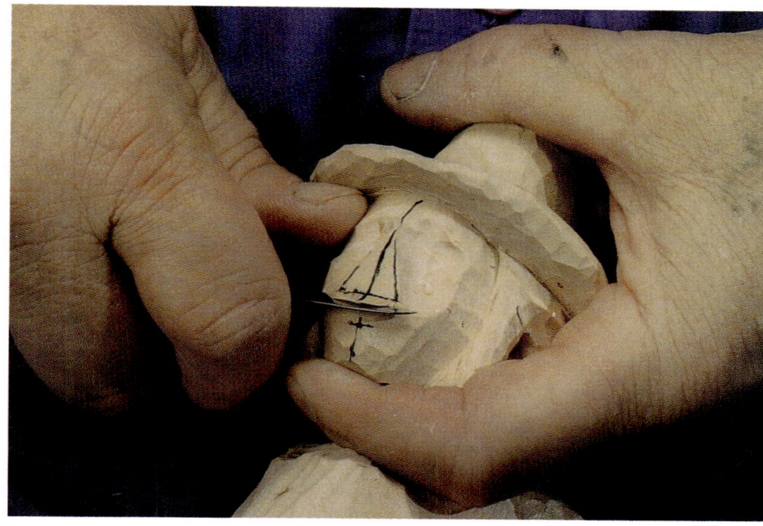

Another stop cut from underneath. The nose can be as long as you'd like it.

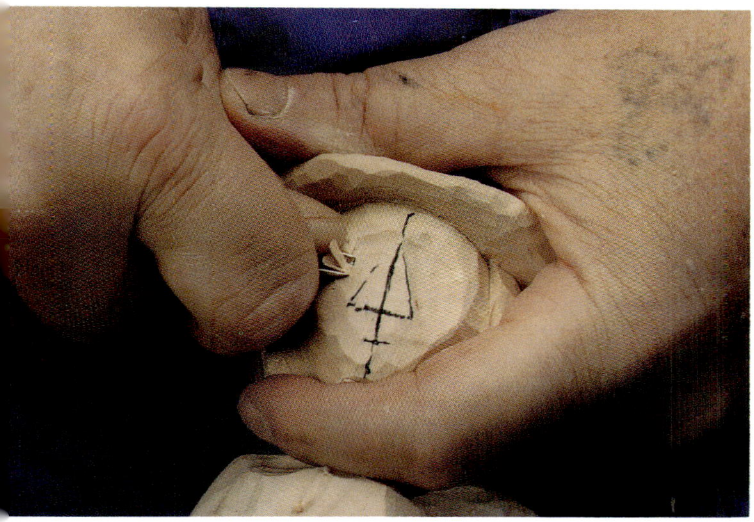

A good rule of thumb is that if the nose looks too big, make it a little bigger. If the eyes are the window to the face, than the nose is the doorknob.

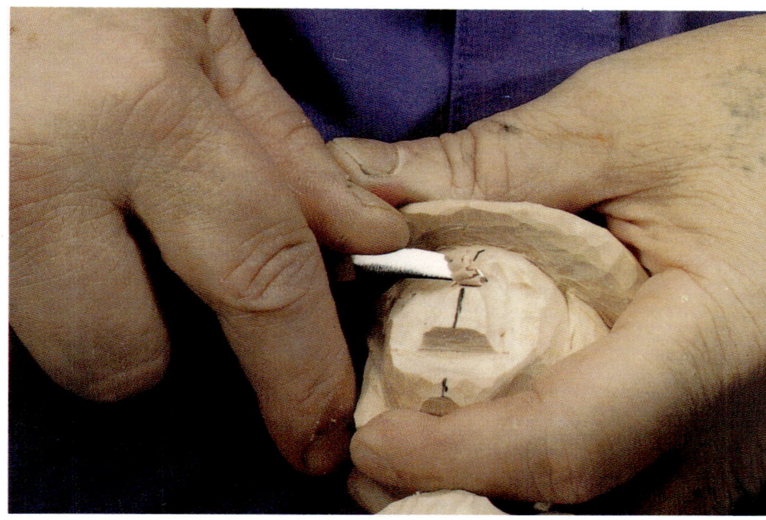

Working out the bridge of the nose a bit. At this stage you want the face free of marks or anything that might mess up your perspective.

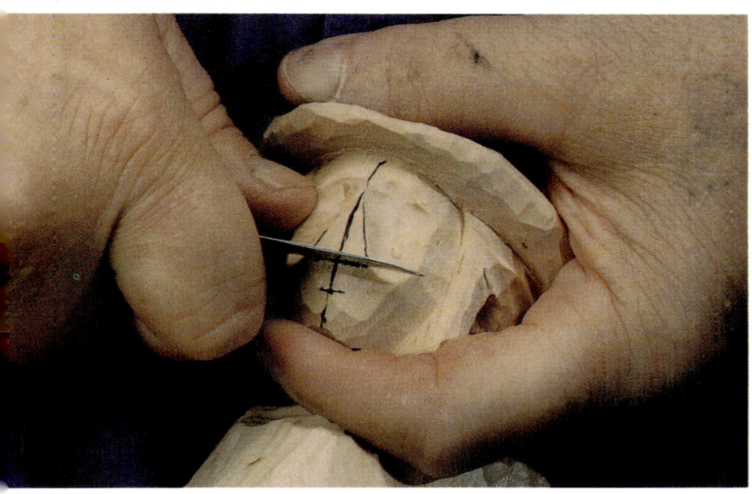

Make a stop cut for the bottom of the nose. Just apply pressure and rock back and forth, and the blade goes in deeper.

Now we can see a profile.

Draw the feet on the bottom of the figure. Because I would like to avoid that mark made by the duplicator, I'll turn one foot to the side.

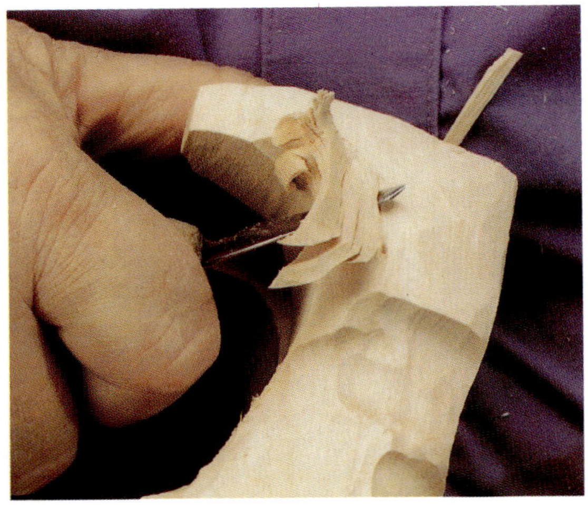

I'm using stop cuts here to make sure the wood doesn't break.

Remember to make the feet pretty large if the figure has no base.

Progress. To keep the legs the right shape, I aim for an octagon shape, making flat planes and then cutting the corners on the angles. I'm keeping the legs as full as possible to leave room for the waders.

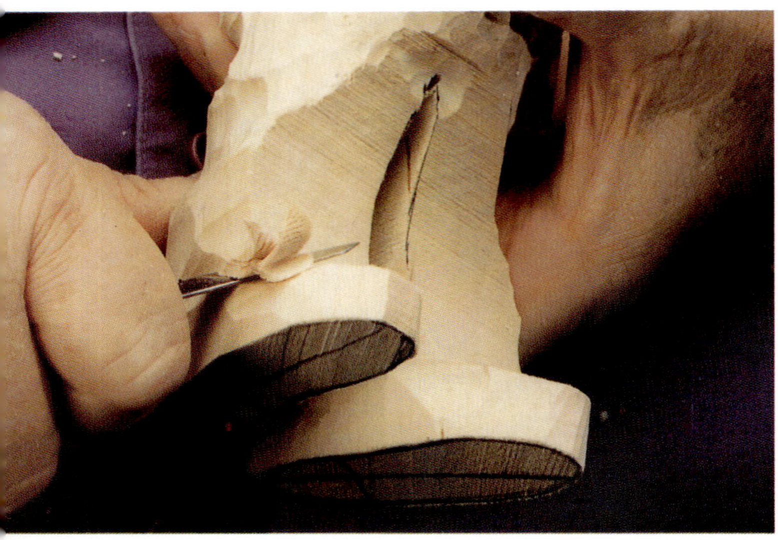

I can cut all of this wood down to the size of the shoe soles, because the legs will come out of that.

Progress.

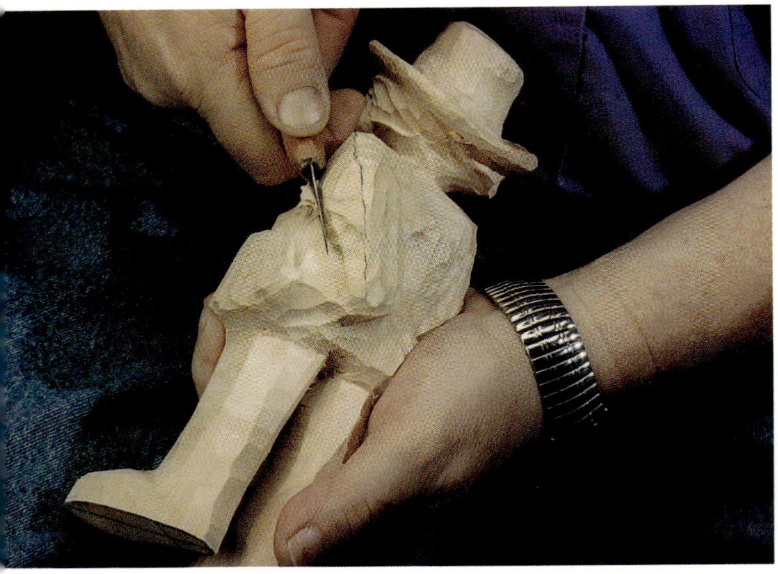

To make the arm, I'll first draw a line to make sure it stays straight, and then make straight cuts on both sides of it.

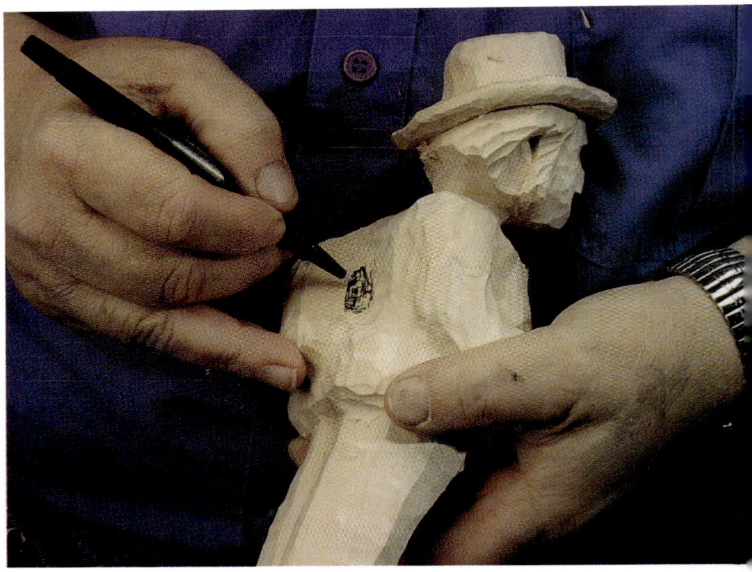

This is what I'm going to take out of the arm to bring it away from the body. I've marked both sides. Don't take off too much yet.

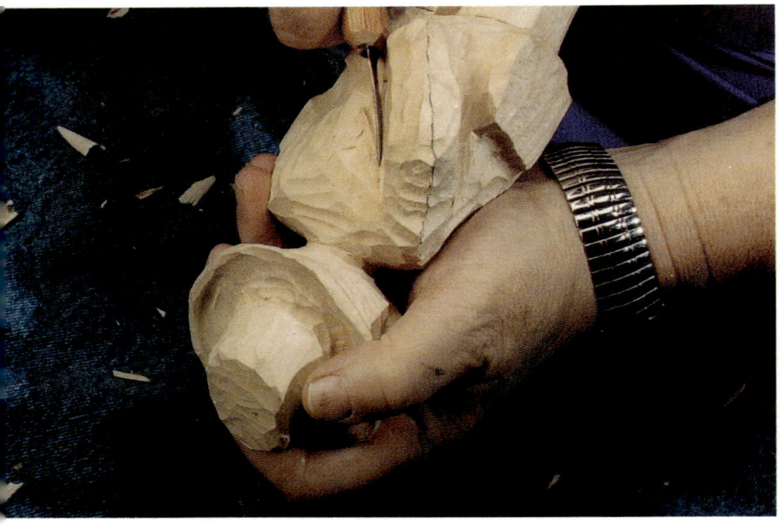

Finishing the arm.

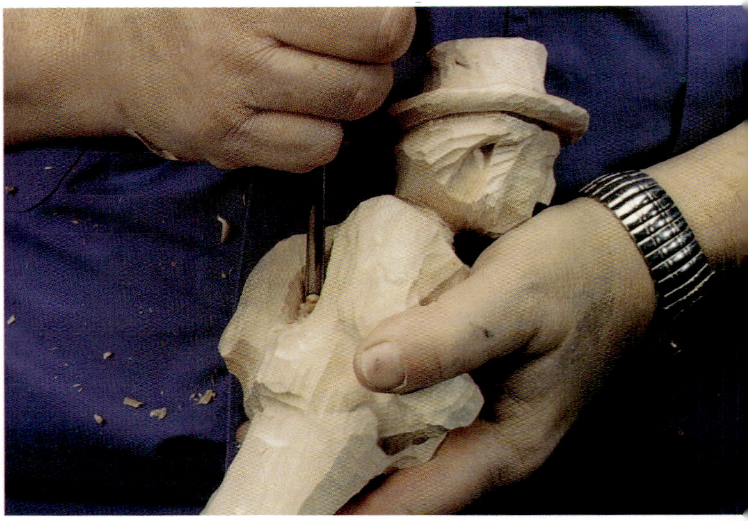

I'm using a gouge, working from both sides to meet in the middle. You can use a drill to do the same thing, but be careful—that's an easy way to make a big mistake!

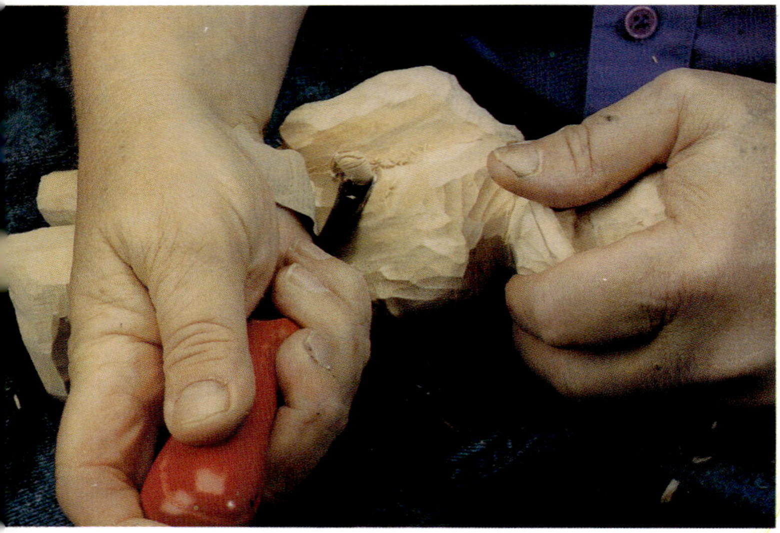

Since his belly paunches out in front, I'm swaying his back, which also leaves more room to work on that arm.

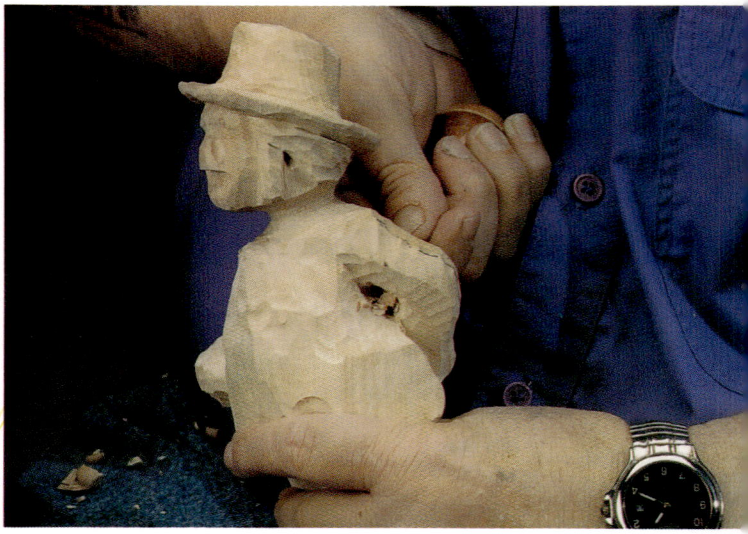

Progress.

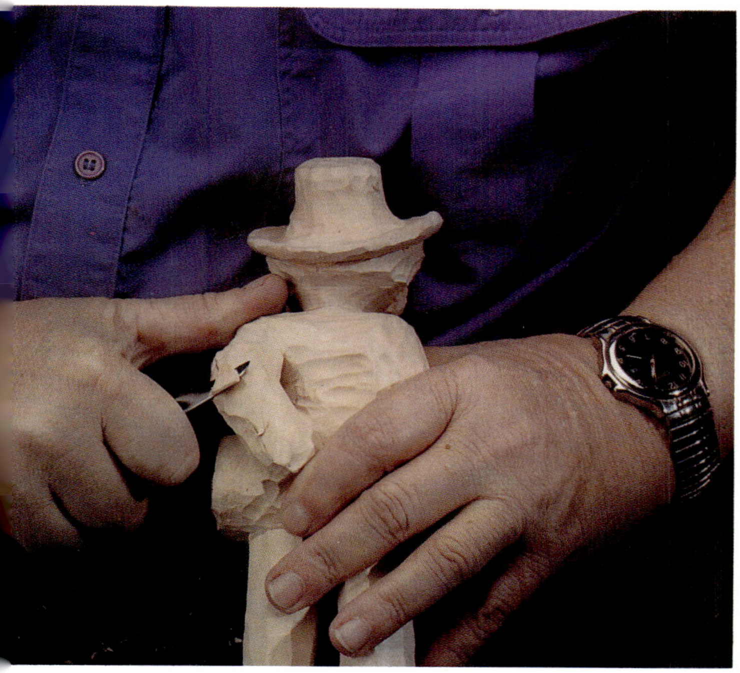

I'm using a knife now to take a little more off. The knife reaches sharp areas the gouge can't.

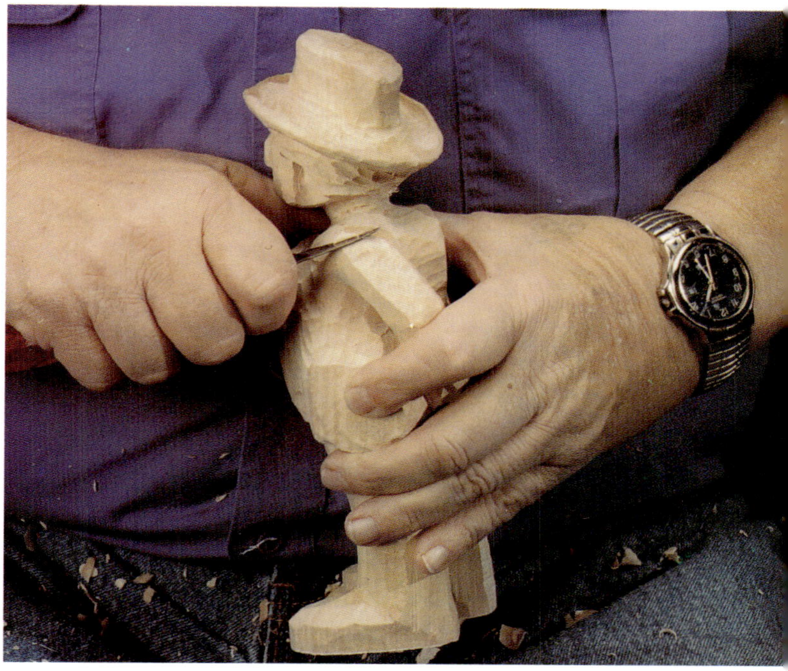

The more I think about it, the more I want the head turned slightly to line up with the turned foot. To do that I will detatch the head, so I'm going to have to make more neck to be able to put it back on again. That means his shoulder needs to come down. Remember that the shoulder is in line right with the side of the body.

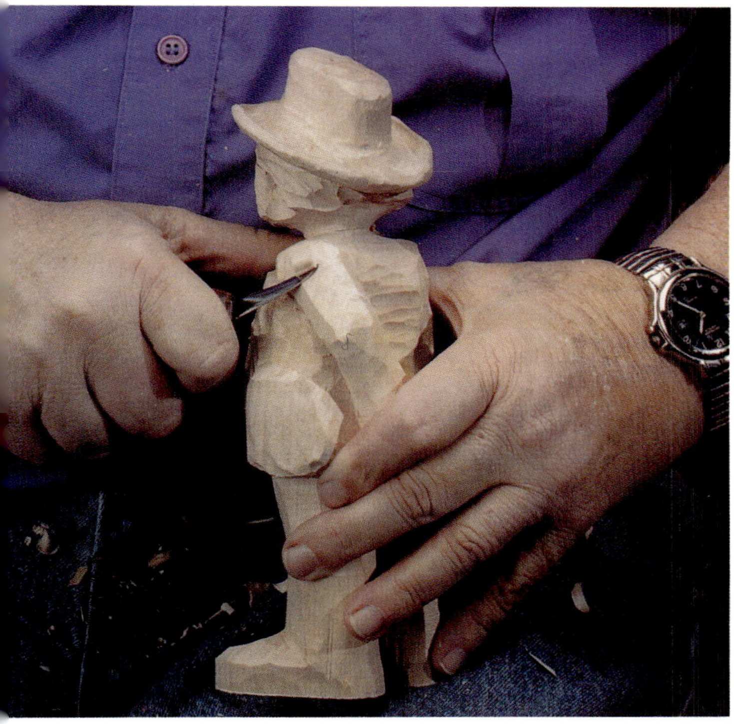

I'll shape the arm using the octagon much like I did with the legs, keeping the angle of the elbow.

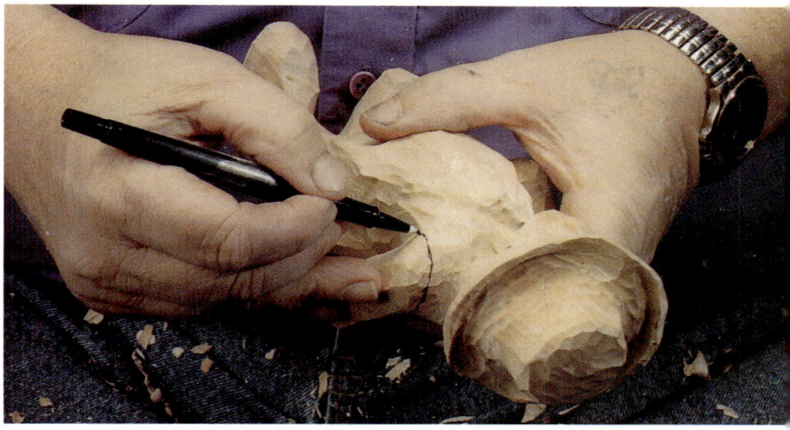

It helps to mark the shoulder line to make sure it doesn't come out too far.

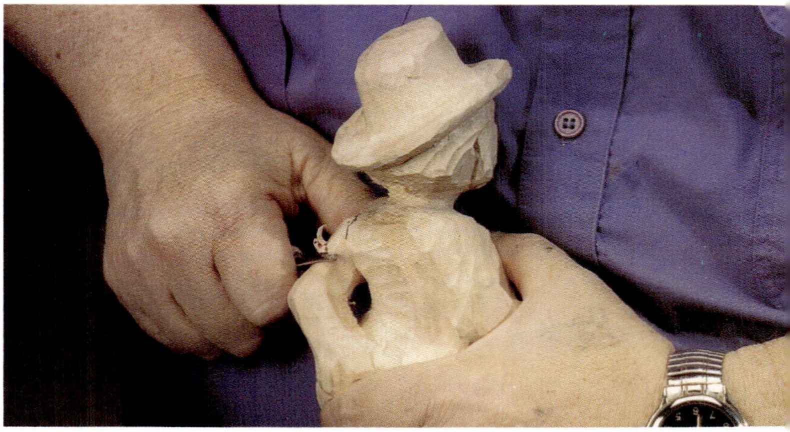

Now that we've reestablished the shoulder, we also need to reestablish the arm.

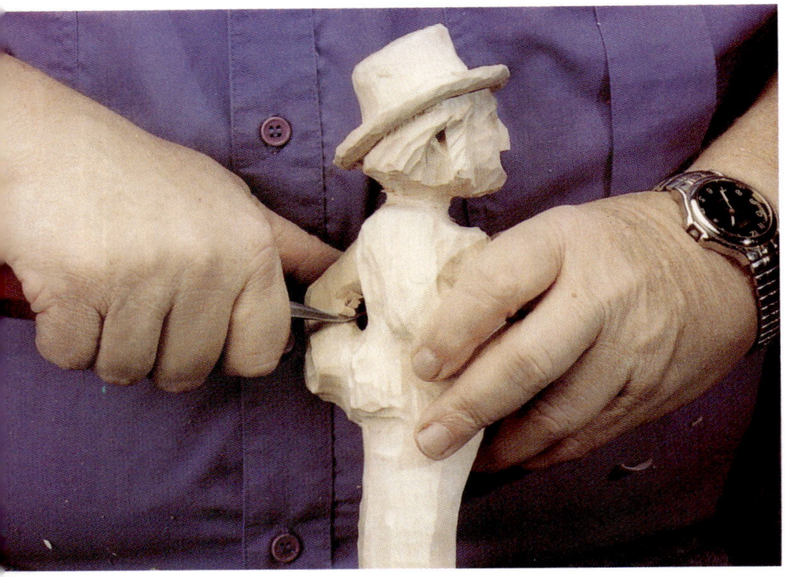

There's also a new outer angle for the elbow, so we need to realign the inner one.

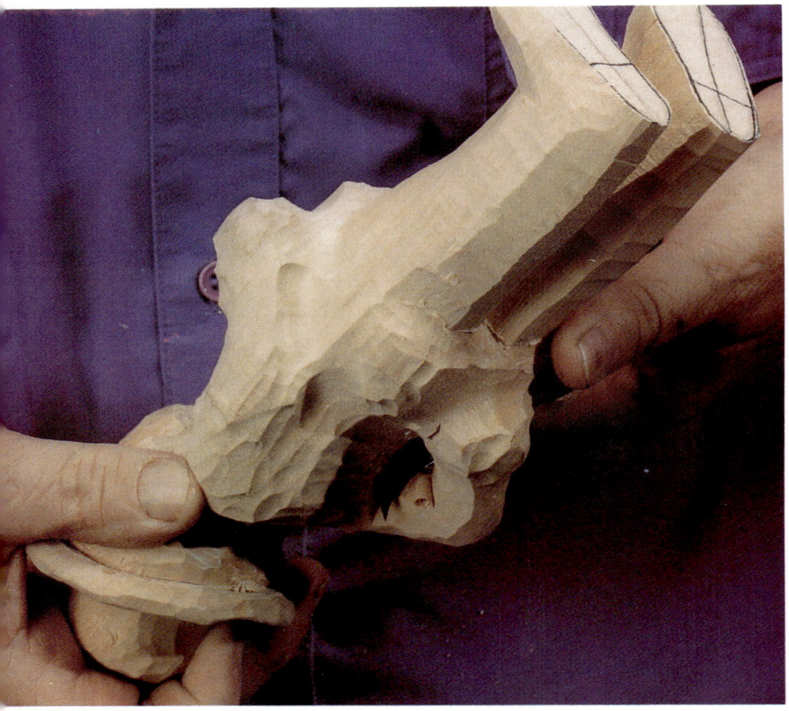

Progress. My hooked knife is perfect for these types of cuts.

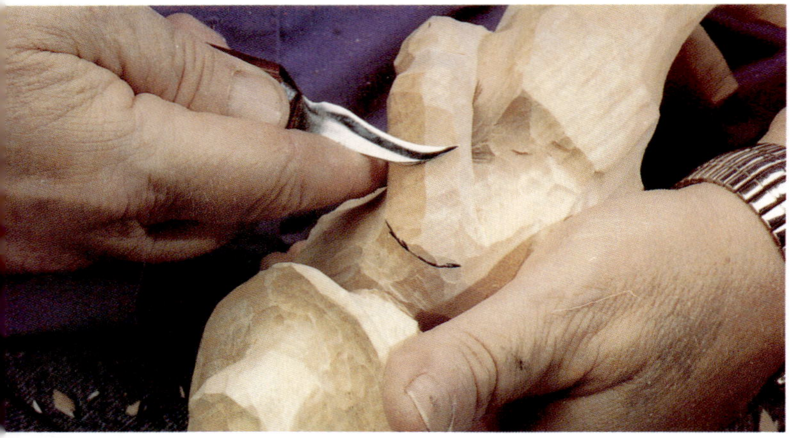

Use this arm and the knife blade...

...as a reference to size the other arm.

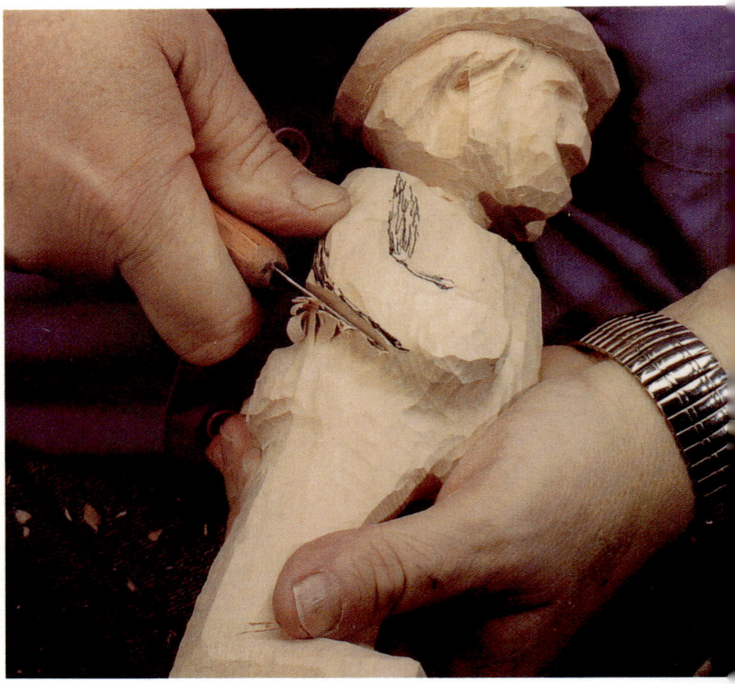

I've marked the part I need to cut away. I'm using square cuts to bring the arm out nice and heavy.

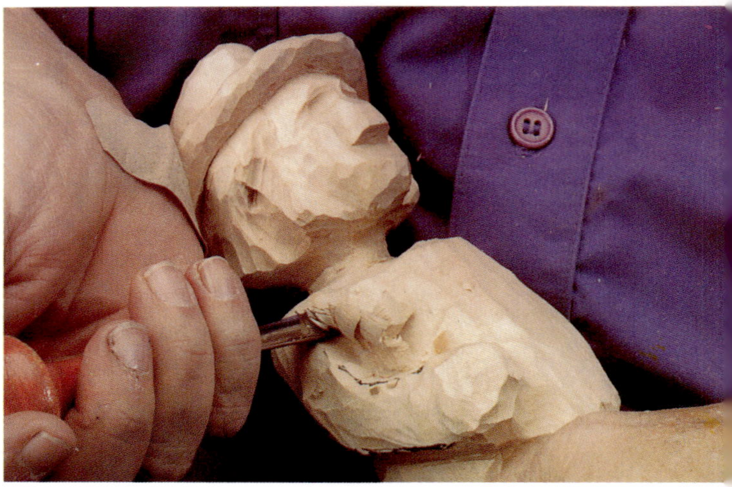

It needs to be the same thickness on both sides.

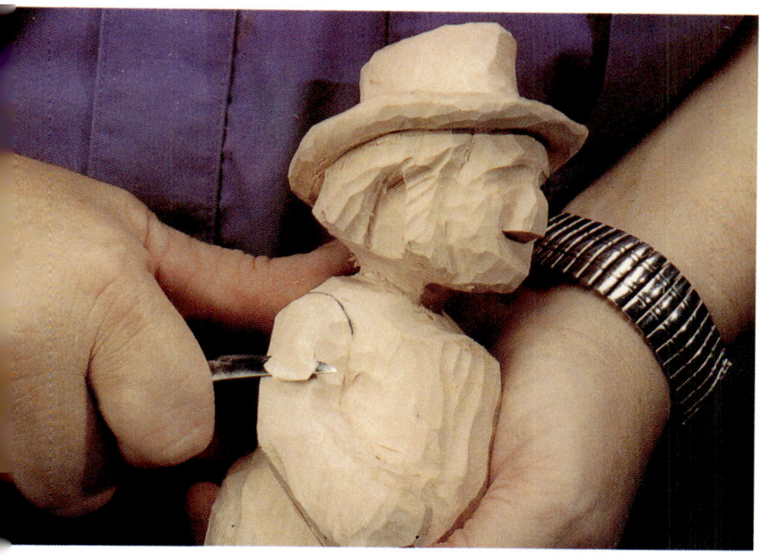

I think the shoulder needs to come down now. That means I'll have to bring it in closer to the body and drop the elbow so the arm stays in proportion.

Since I need to lengthen the neck, I will go ahead and cut out the ears. Rememer that the ear lobe needs to be on the same line as the bottom of the nose.

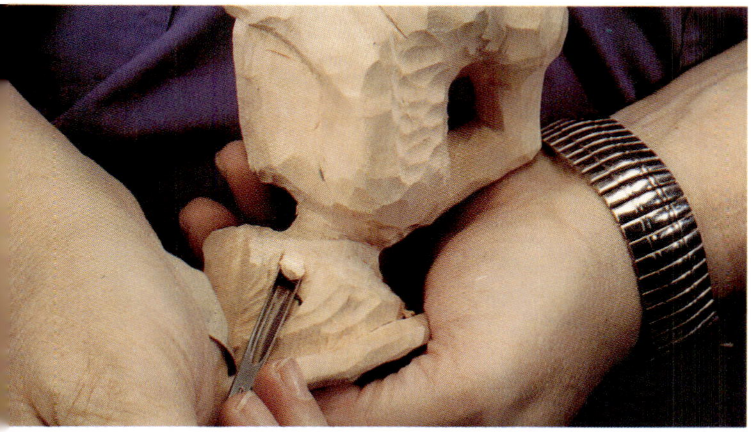

Using a half-round gouge, I'm working down away from the ear so it blends into the neck.

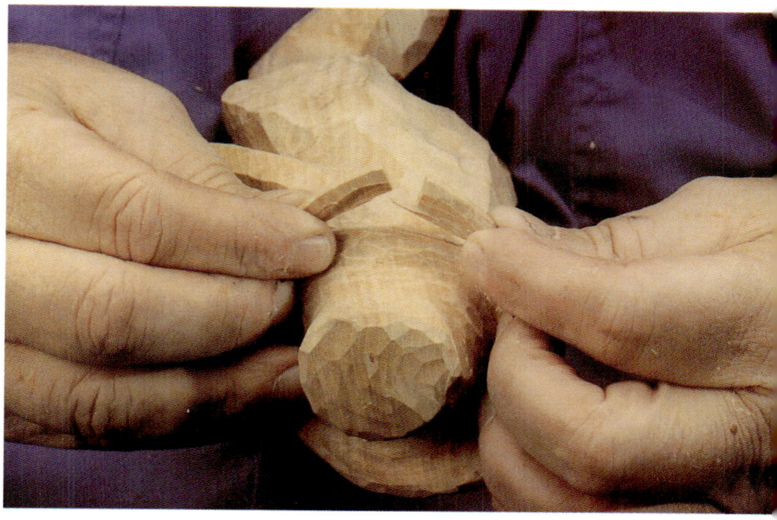

See, I told you not to put so much pressure on the hat! We'll use some glue to fix the problem. Regular white glue is fine, because stronger glue can dry too fast and make an even bigger problem. Put the pieces back on starting with the ones closest to the solid figure, matching the grain as closely as possible. Allow plenty of drying time.

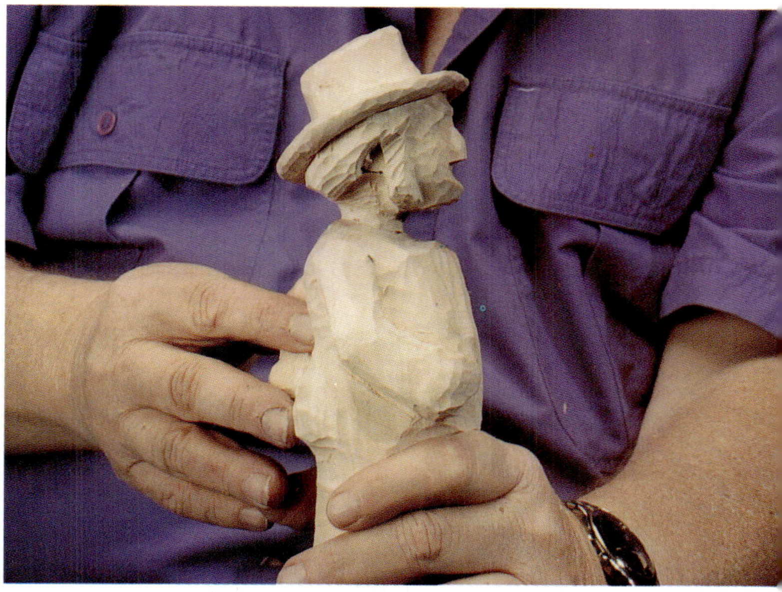

Back to the head. Every bit of extra length in the neck helps, because it leaves more room to fit it back on the shoulders.

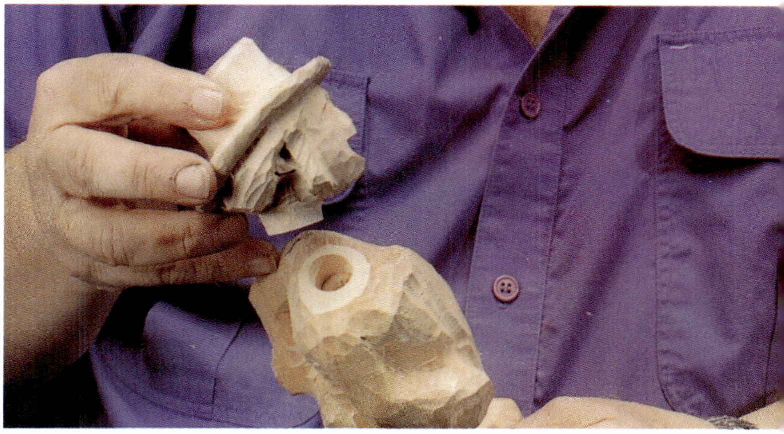

I cut the head off with a bandsaw and drilled a hole in the figure with a drill press. The hole needs to match the size of the neck pretty closely.

A good way to size the hole is to work the neck into it. Look for the shiny spots where the wood really rubs; that's what needs to be cut back. Be careful not to make the hole too big or the neck too skinny.

Progress.

The neck looks a little short—I'm going to bring the shoulders down some more.

I'm making a series of straight cuts with a knife to round the arm and bring it away from the body.

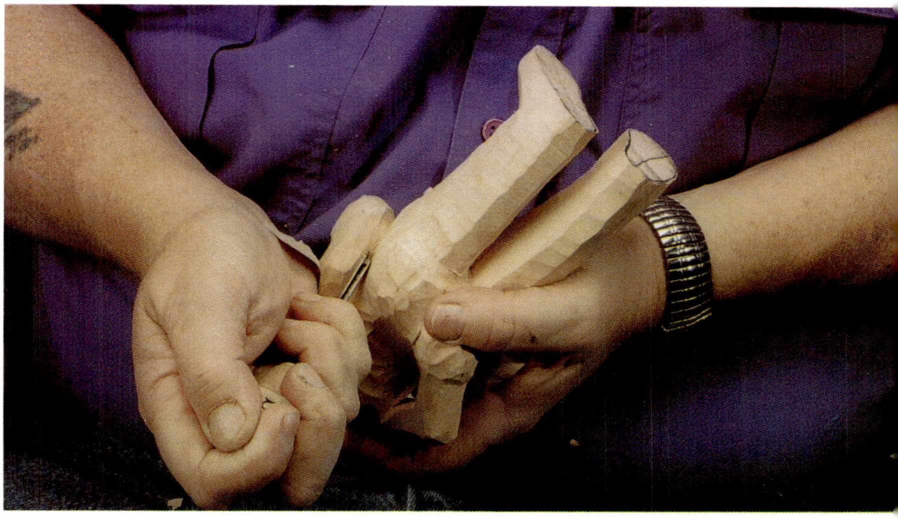

I'm using a 24° V-Tool by Charles Berold to clean up the groove. The same thing could be done with two careful cuts of the knife.

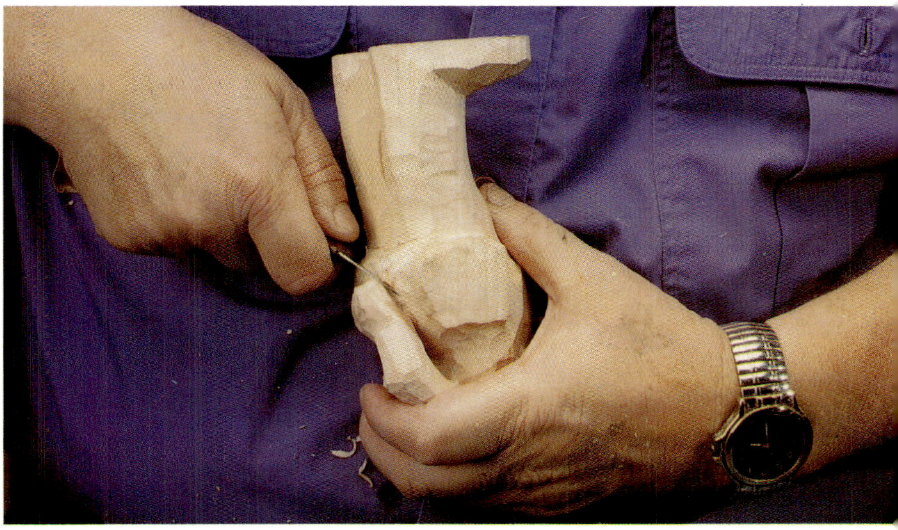

I'm bringing the hands out, but I'm leaving them big and clubby to make sure there's room for the hole I'll be drilling there.

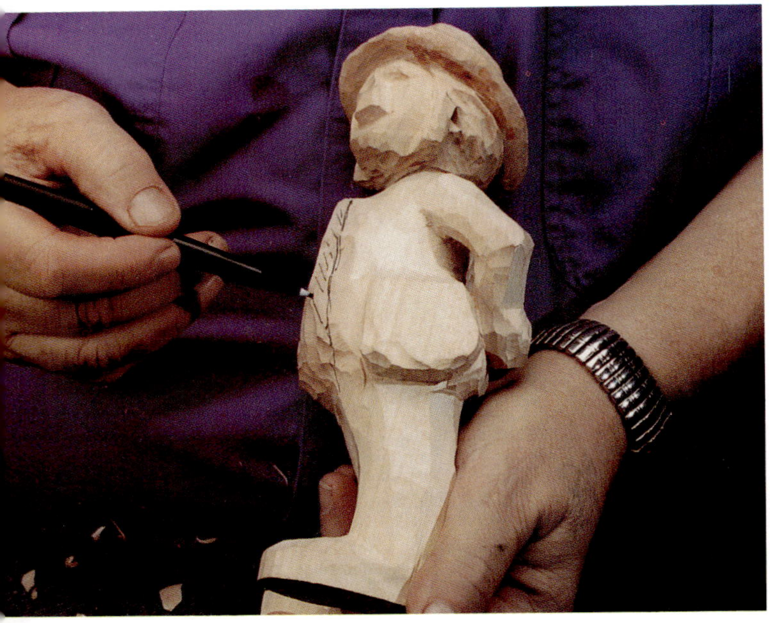

Another thing that would help the short neck is to trim off his belly a little.

Now he's lost about 40 pounds! If you decide to detatch the head like I did, put it back on periodically to make sure everything's in proportion.

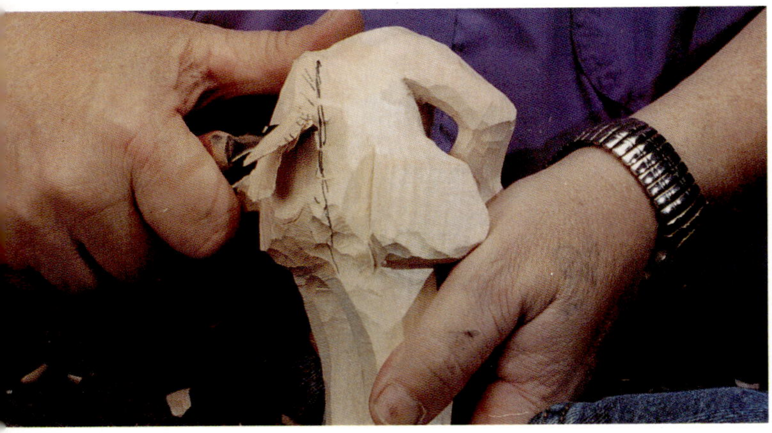

I'm cutting upward with the grain, letting the pieces pop right off.

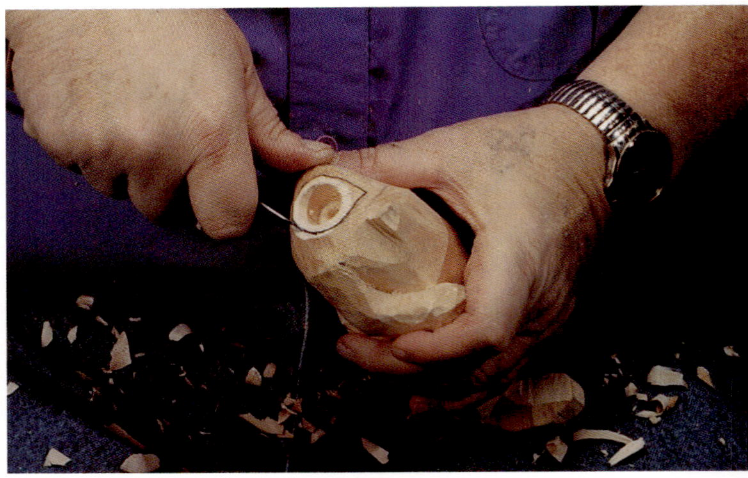

Mark the line for the collar and make a stop cut all the way around.

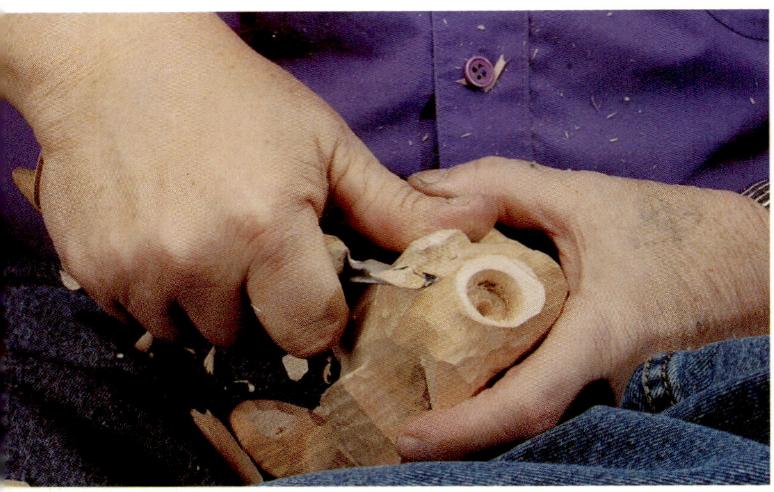

The fisherman needs a strap for his creel, so I'm leaving some wood for it.

A clean groove brings the collar away from the neck and makes a nice clean line for painting.

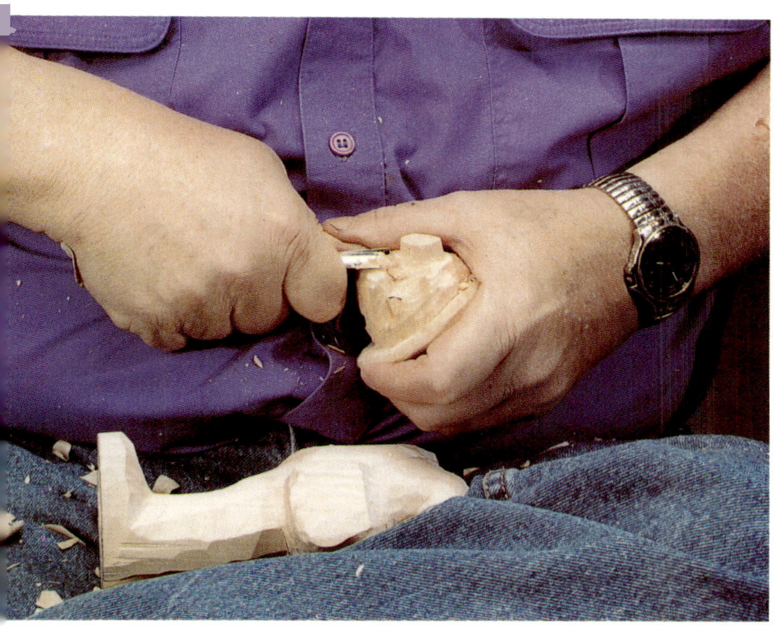

Since I have some room on the head, I'm moving the neck line up a little by undercutting the sideburns and hairline.

Progress on the collar, strap, and tie.

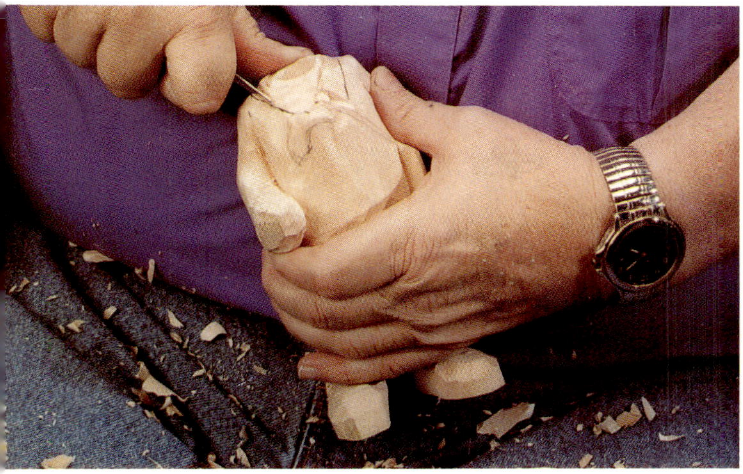

When you think about the clothing for the figure, make sure the outer layer is the first cut. Here we have the collar on top, the strap next, and the tie underneath.

Now that I look at it, I see that the collar is lopsided. I want to make the short side longer.

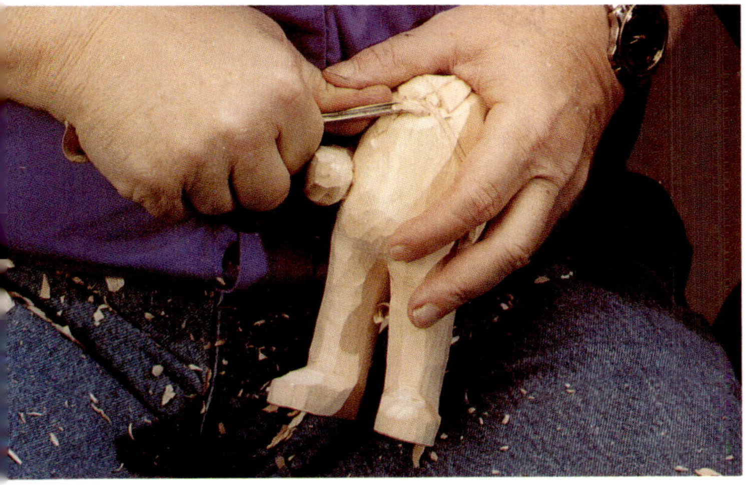

The tie will be bunched from the strap. I'm using a veiner to make the folds.

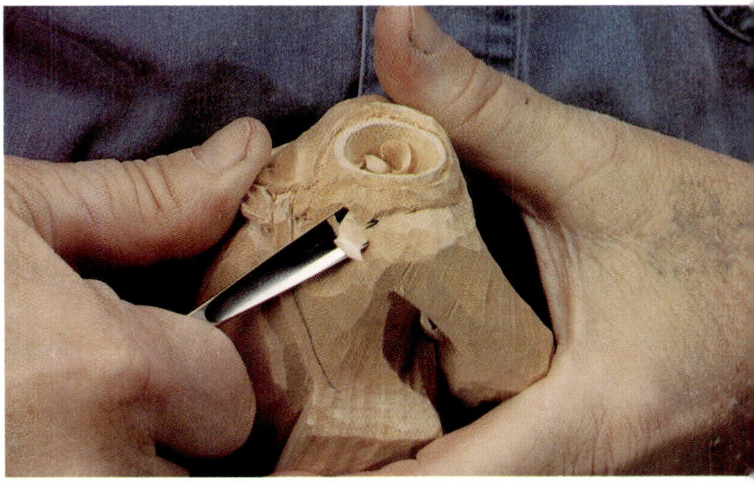

Smooth out the existing collar.

Make a stop cut where the new collar line should be. Then cut back to it from underneath.

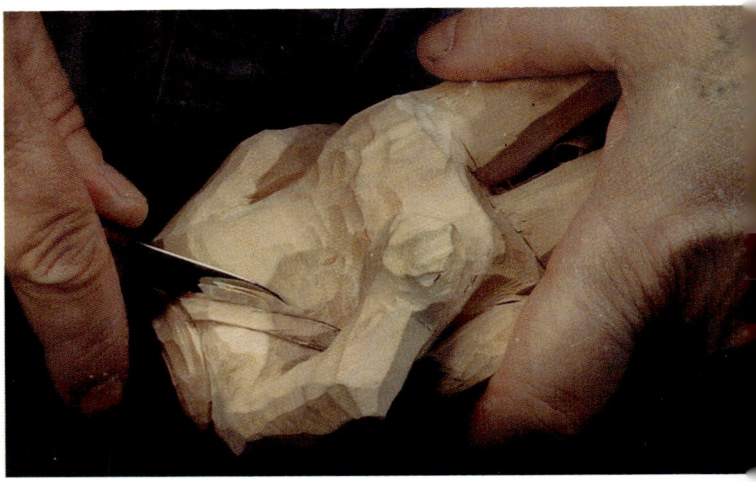

Make sure you cut one side at a time, in case there's a mis-cut; then you can balance it out.

While I'm at it, I'm going to make the strap for the creel a little thicker. Use another stop cut and work down to it.

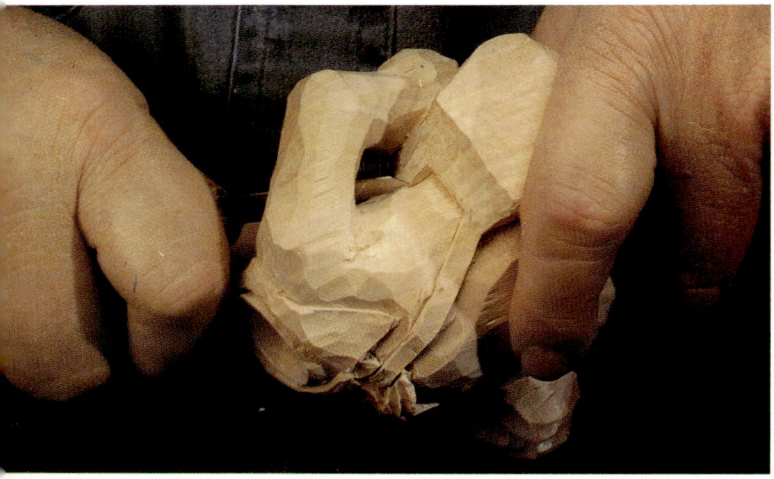

Now I need to define the creel itself and bring the strap up the back over the shoulder. Cut a stop all the way around to the shoulder.

Progress. Now we can start work on the rest of the clothing.

He should have a nice heavy trout fishing vest.

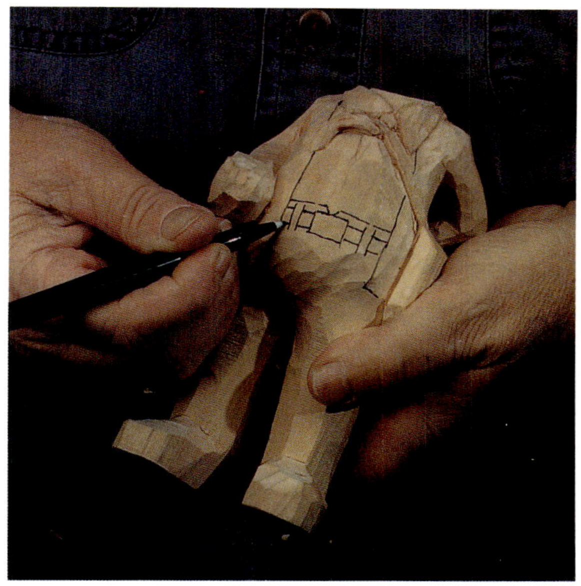

Remember to work from the outside layer of clothing in. Next we have a belt, but we need to remember that the belt-loops will be on top.

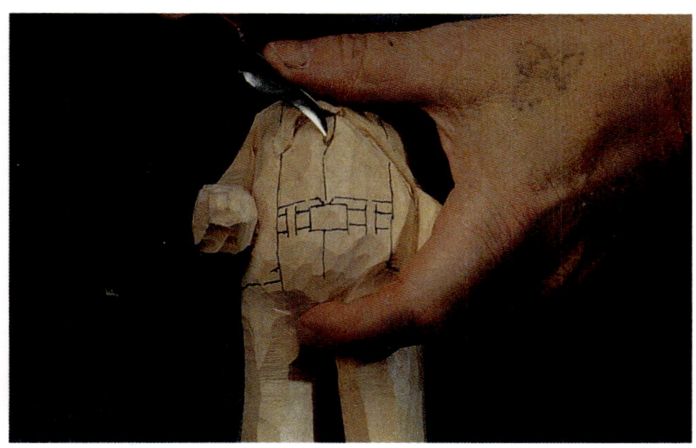

Make the stop cuts clean and sharp to begin with; that saves a lot of work later. This cut needs to be especially clean, because this is going to be skin where the shirt is coming open. A small, flatter gouge is perfect for this kind of cut.

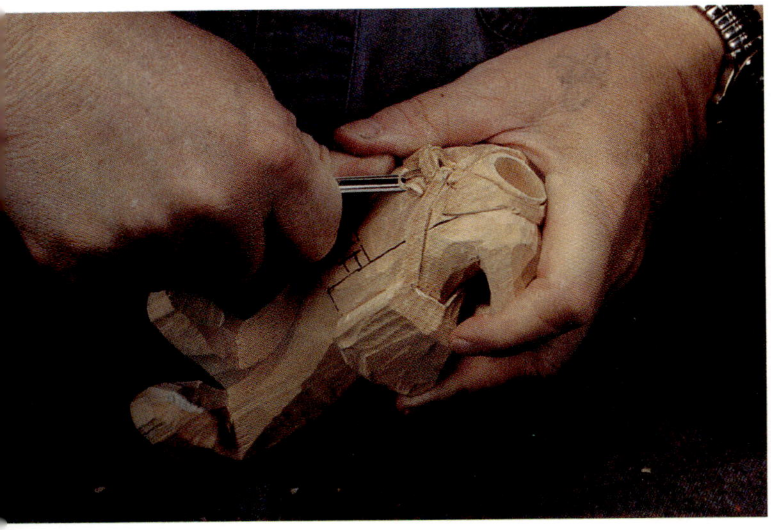

To make a more realistic effect with the shirt, cut away from the edge of the shirt placket, not as deeply as we did with the skin.

I put two cuts in the back of the vest to make a flap. One side will be apart a little to make room for the hook that will be stuck in the seat of his pants.

Then I'll take advantage of this lump on the chest to make the shirt pucker. If you're lost, try scrunching up a real piece of fabric and look at how it folds.

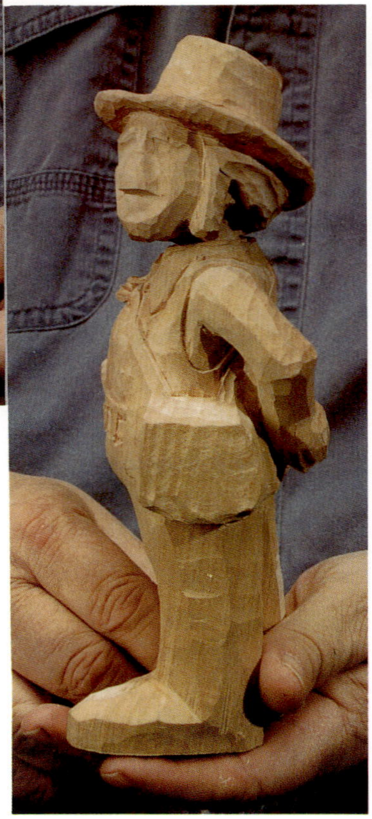

Progress on the clothing.

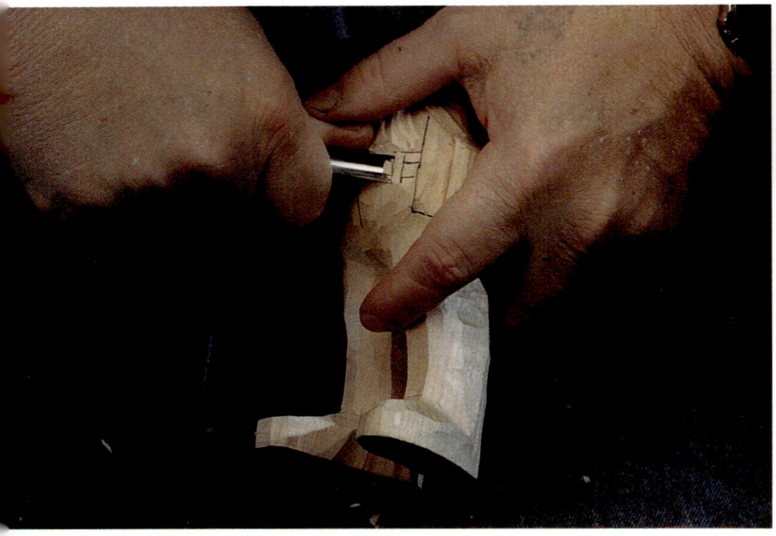

Little details like these belt-loops make a great carving out of a mediocre one.

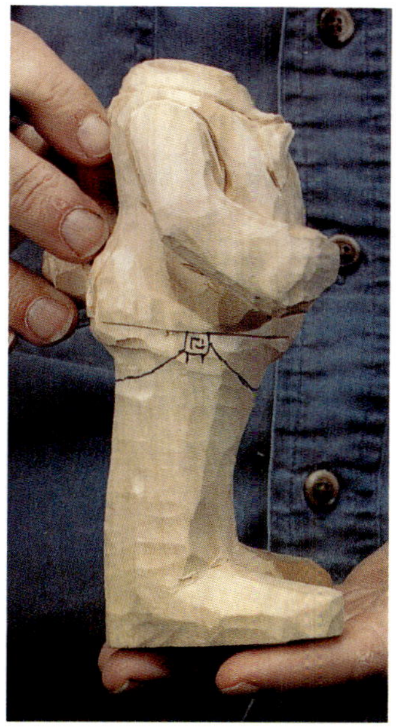

Now let's work on the hip boots.

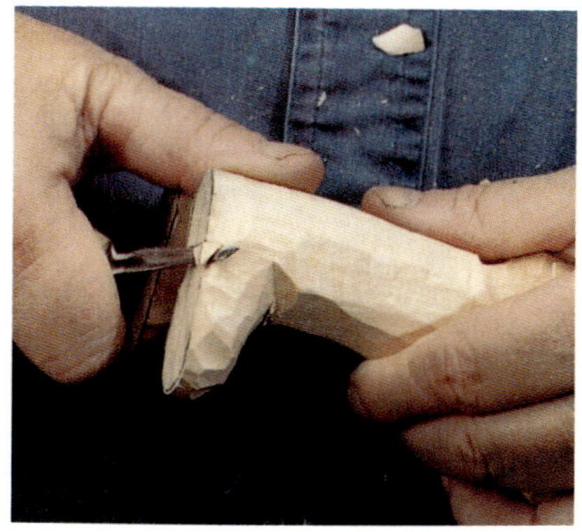

To give the feet more shape, I'm notching out a heel on each side. Don't go all the way across the bottom of the shoe; better to keep it level underneath for balance or gluing.

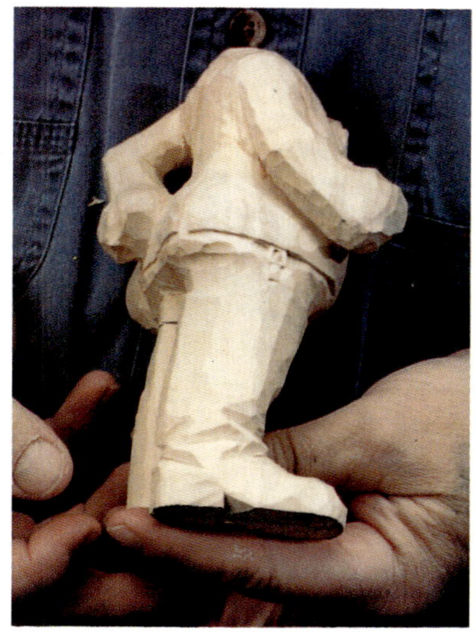

Since hip boots usually sag, I made notches with a knife (with two 45° cuts for each one) that alternate, giving an accordion effect.

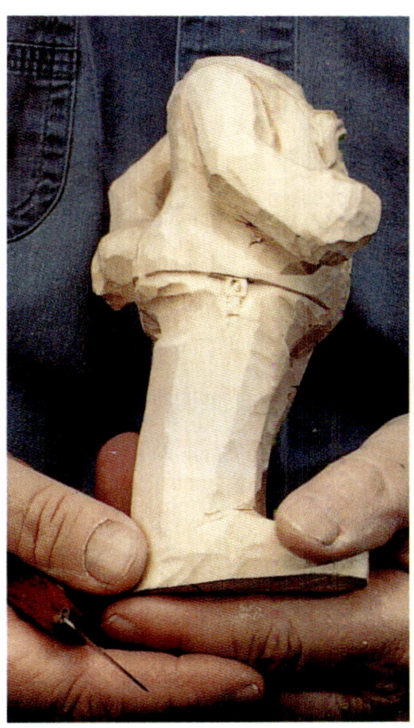

Progress. I'm making stop cuts and then making straight cuts toward them.

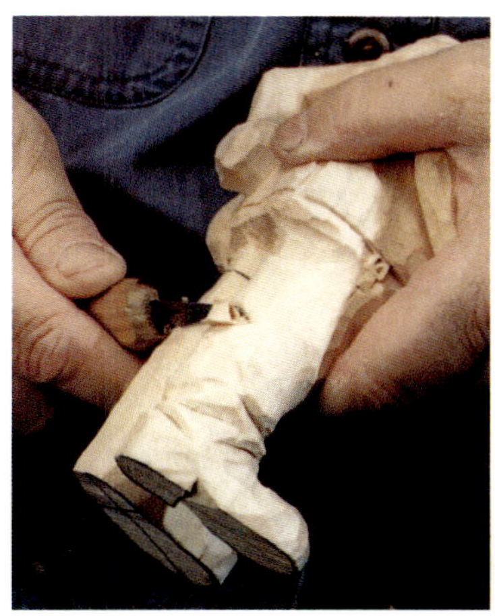

I'm doing the same thing with the back of the knee. One cut up, one cut down.

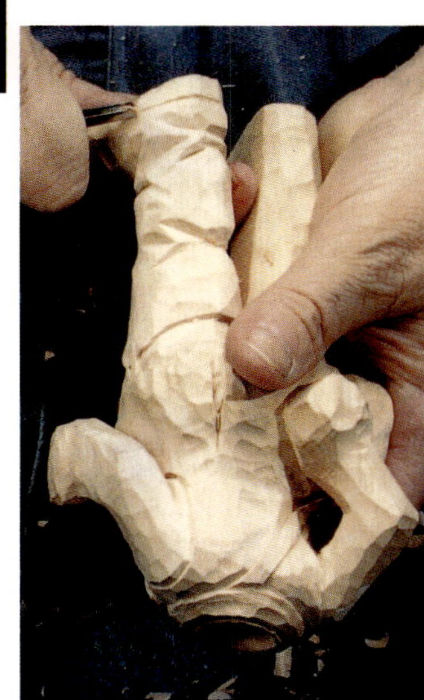

That 24° V-tool is handy for making a deep cut around the foot for the sole of the shoe. It does what two knife cuts could do.

Progress. Here's looking at you!

The longer smoothing cuts can sometimes distract the eye from the true lines of the figure, so it's good to break them up as much as possible. That also cleans up wood that may have gotten dirty from so much handling.

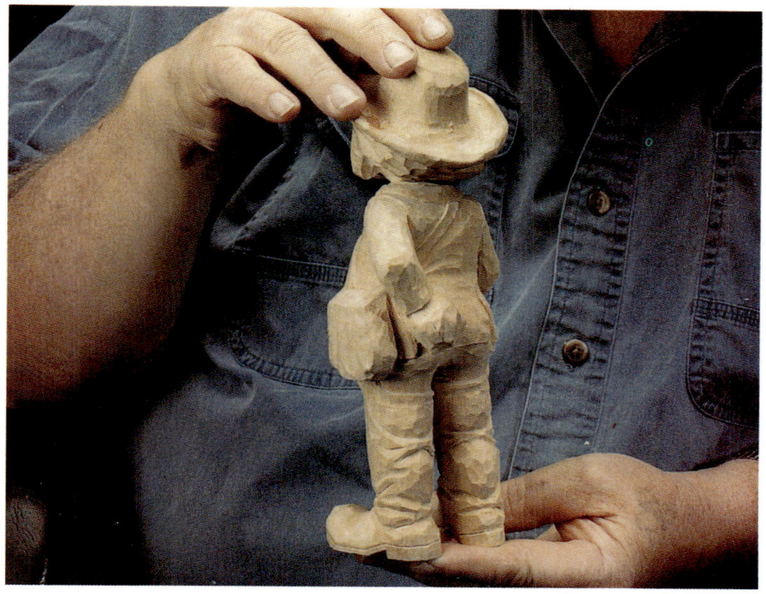

Progress on the body.

The shirt needs cuffs which begin with a stop cut. Then cut from the hand toward the cuff, making the wrist look thinner.

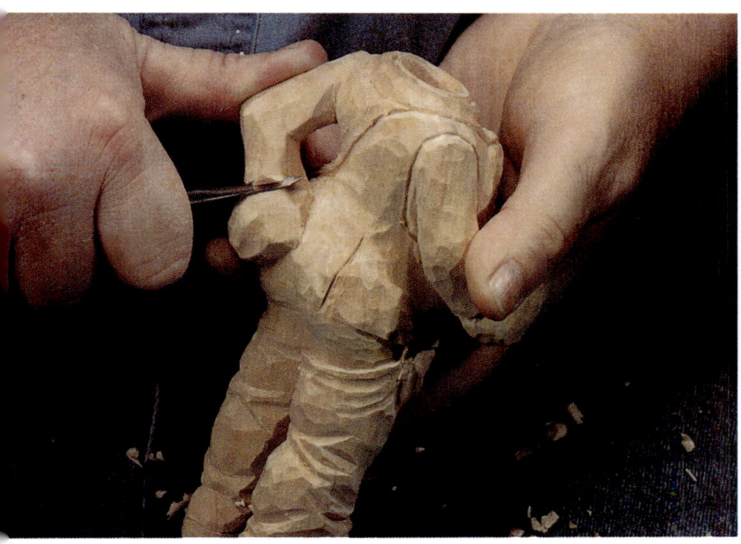

The other hand.

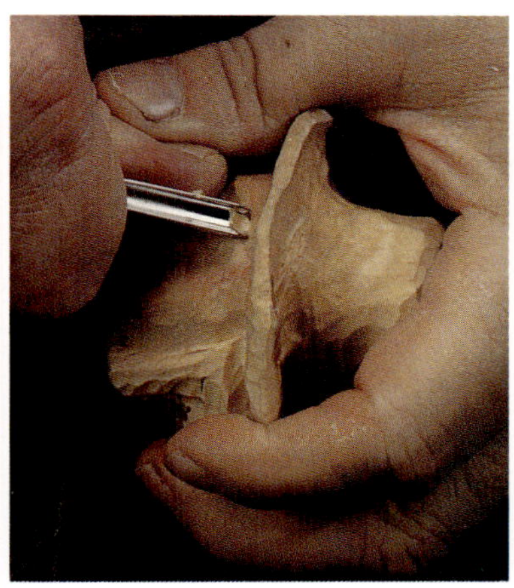

The body looks pretty good. Now we can go back to the head. We'll start by separating the eyebrows.

Make 45° angle nitches on each side of the nose and nip them off. Now we have a full silhouette of the nose, and we can make it look any way we want from here.

Make small vertical cuts right above the nostril cuts we made. These start the smile line.

Make another cut 45° upward from that cut...

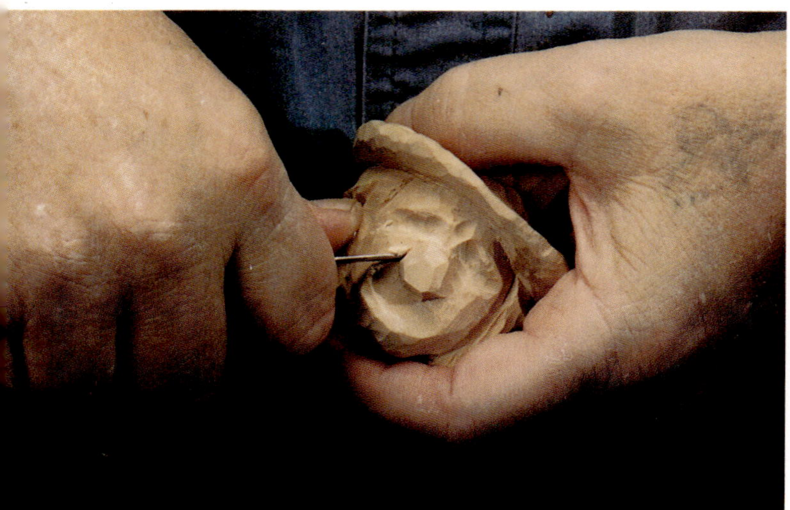

...and make a third one to make a triangle. Pop that little piece out.

These cuts are a triangle-shaped foundation for cheeks, lips, or a moustache.

Bring the nose marks down around the mouth, not too deeply. Make sure the nose stays rounded and clean.

Since he's just found himself in a bad position, he should have an uncomfortable look on his face. I'll start by making a cut straight across that angles down a little bit on one side.

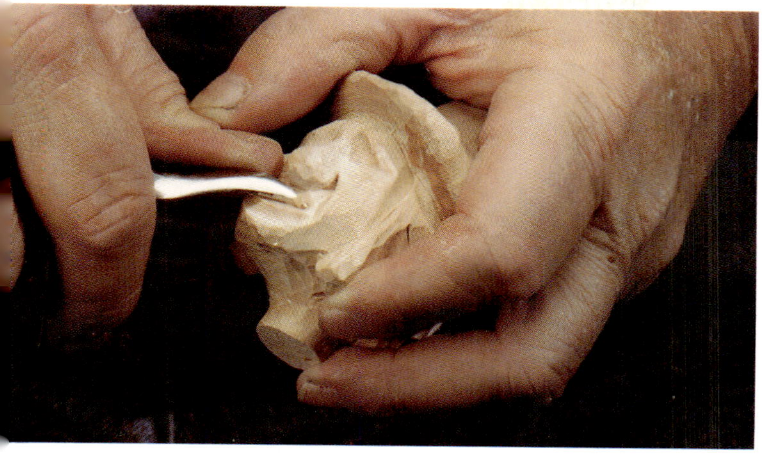

I'm cutting the corners of the mouth deeper, as the part in between could be teeth or tongue. I think I'll go with a tongue.

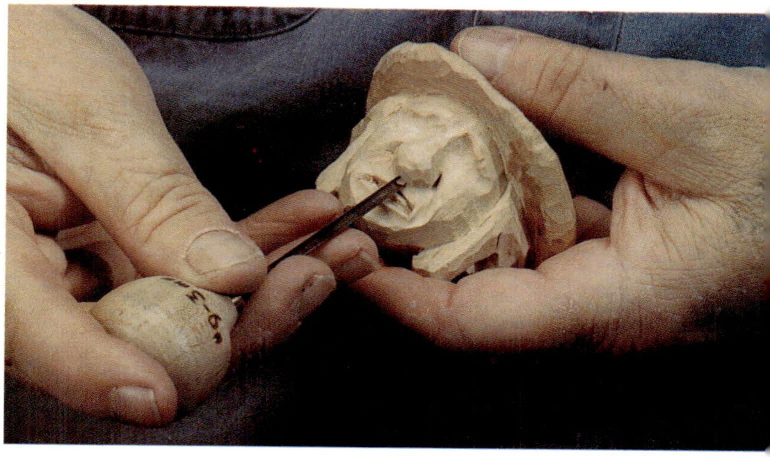

One cut with a small half round gouge makes the philtrum, that divet under the nose.

I've decided on teeth *and* a tongue. The center line between the lips serves as both the top of the teeth and the bottom of the tongue.

We need a little curve to the lip now.

I'm using the hooked knife to separate the teeth.

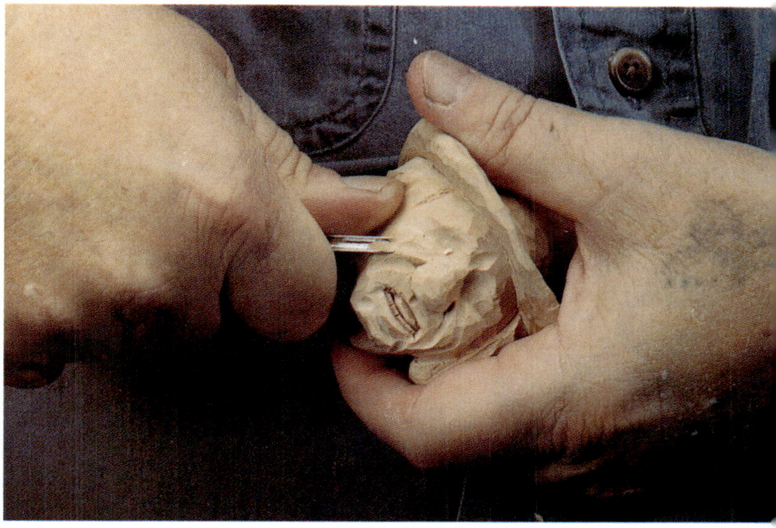

Let's add some character lines behind that first curve we made around the mouth. I'm using a small half round gouge.

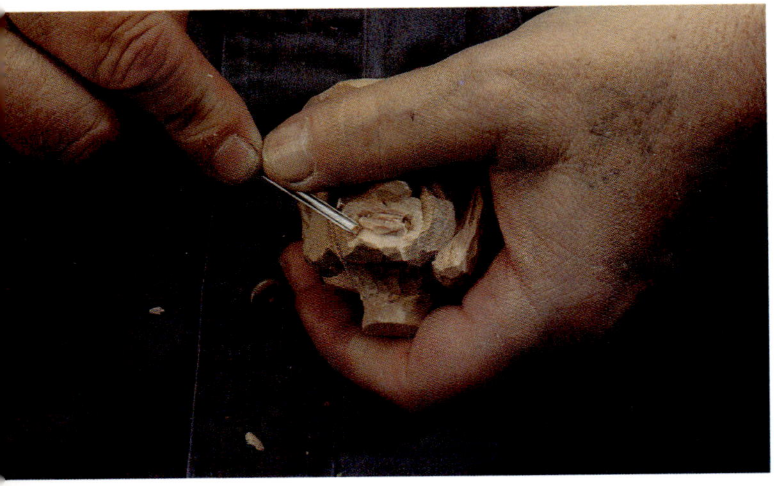

The lips come together, but it always looks like the lower lip goes under the upper one a little. I like to make a shadow line here with a couple of little cuts at the corner of the mouth.

One cheek is a little larger than the other, so I need to cut it down some toward the sideburn.

Now for the ear. Start with an undercut to make the lobe. Then scoop out a hole for the ear canal. The top of the ear will be covered with hair.

The finished ear.

Moving on to the eyes. I use eye punches for this, even though it's possible to use a knife. The punch is much easier. These are my own design, available from Woodcraft.

Push the punch into the eye socket with a gentle rocking motion.

I'm going to make a cut at the corners of the eyes similar to the ones around the nostrils. Start with a cut downwards from the eye lid,

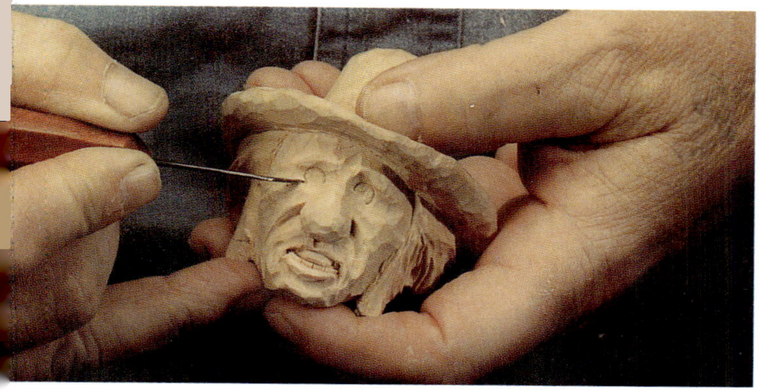

Then make a cut up from underneath,

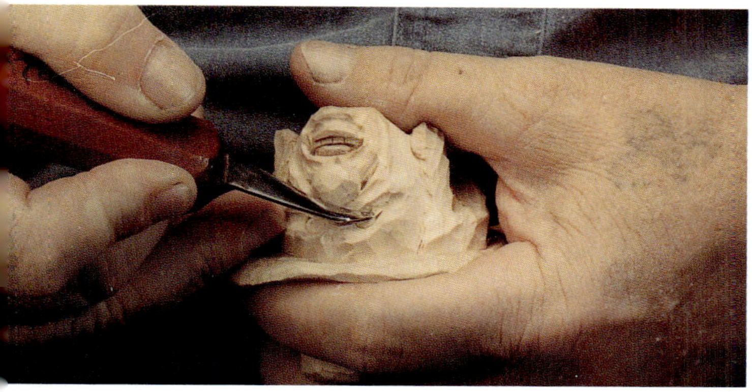

Then one from the eyeball. This is a hooked knife's time to shine.

Progress.

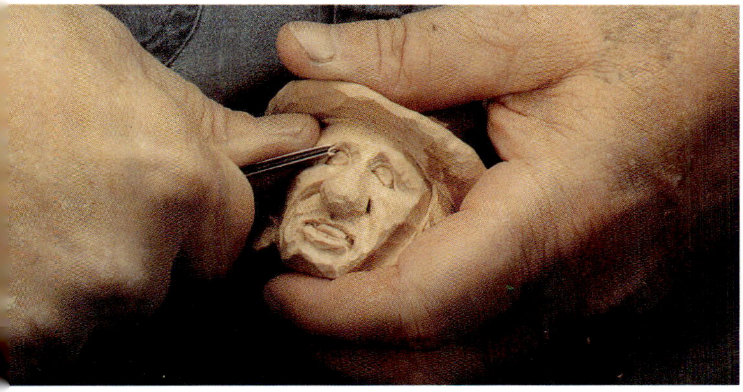

I'm using a small veiner for the eyelids. The name of the game is to make the lids as thin as possible without breaking through to the eye.

Small bags under the eyes also enhance the expression.

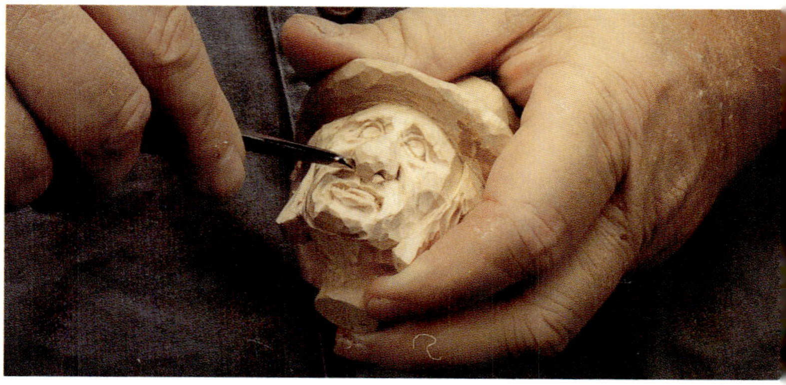

For the nose, I start with the nostril. Use a small half round gouge in a downward motion to make the nostrils. I've learned that it's better to space the nostrils farther apart than on a real nose.

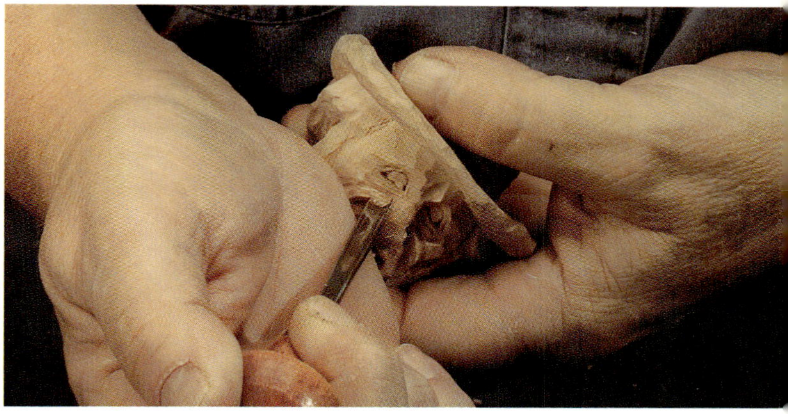

To shape the nose, I start where the flare of the nostril should be, working up and then over into the grain of the face. The pieces come off easily this way.

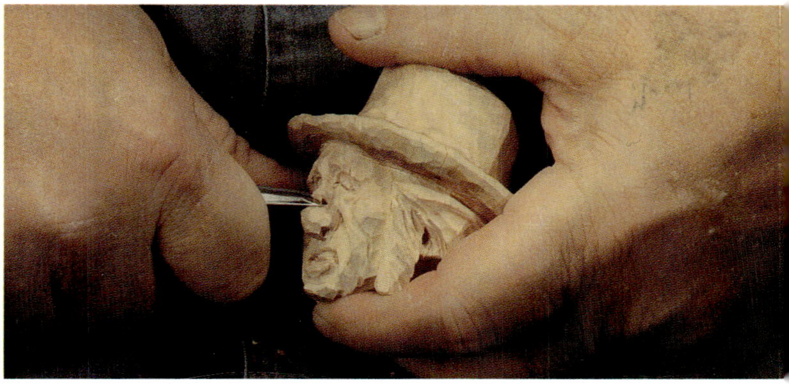

I don't like the shape of the nose, so I'm changing its profile.

The new nose.

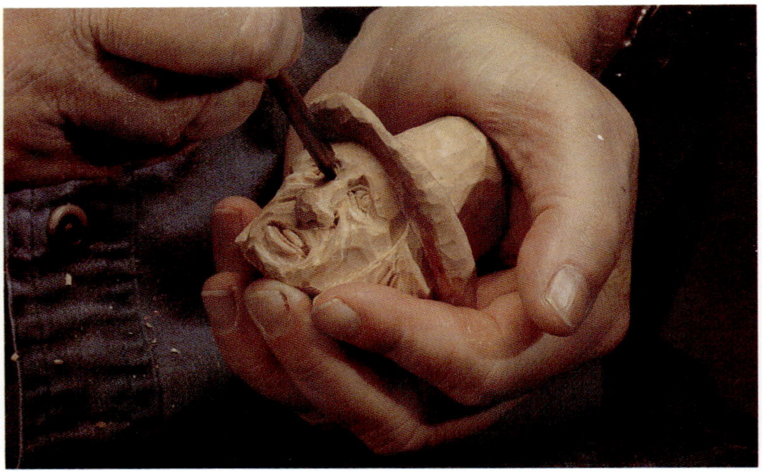

To make the iris in the eye, I'm using a smaller eye punch. Be careful not to use too much pressure and wreck the rest of the eye.

The veiner is good for the eyebrows. Make a series of little cuts from the inside outward.

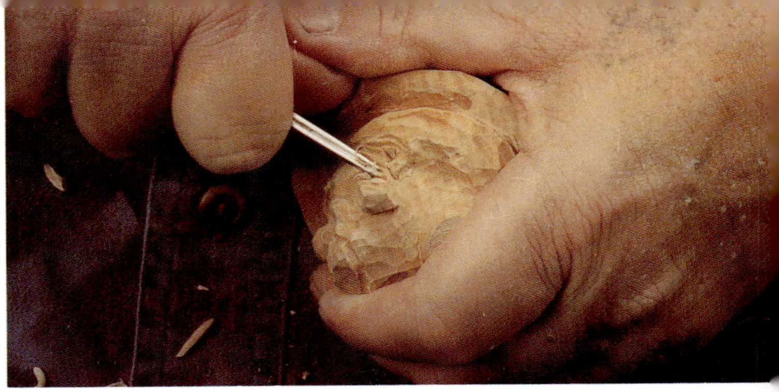

Continue on with the veiner for the sideburns.

The rest of the hair should be different in texture, so I'm using a gouge. You can use a slightly larger gouge to add more variety.

Progress.

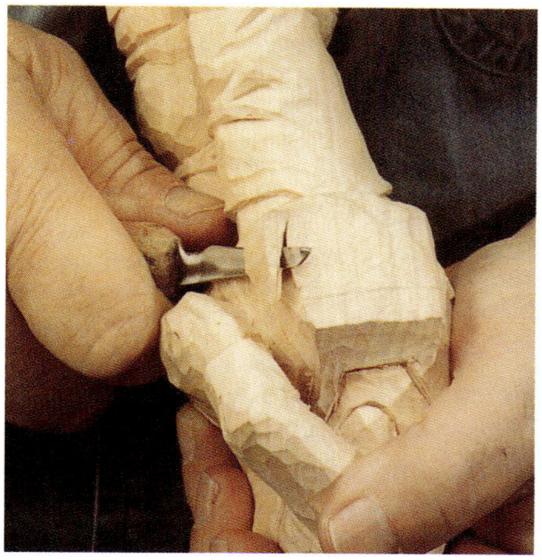

I need to touch up the creel a little bit; it looks lobberjaw.

The creel should be squared off with an angled lid.

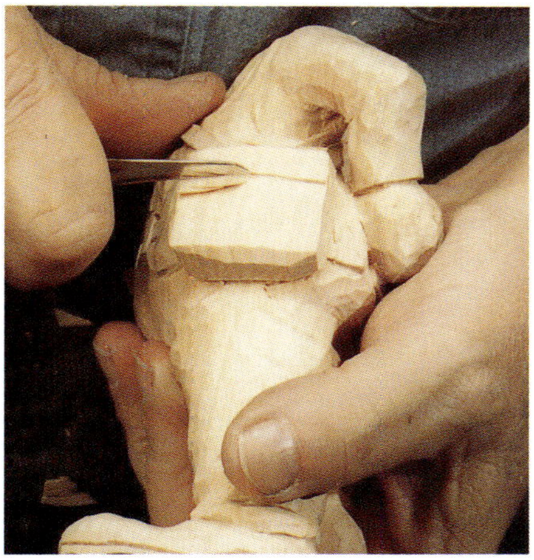

I'm making the lid by starting with a stop cut and cutting up towards it.

The creel has a hole in the top to drop fish through. I'm using the hooked knife to get good deep cuts on the corners.

Make cuts on the sides and dig out the center.

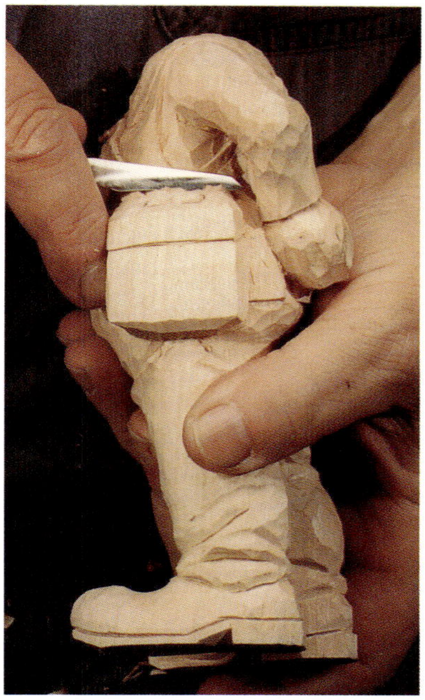

I would like the straps to run out from behind the creel, so I'm cutting out the excess between the strap and lid with two knife cuts.

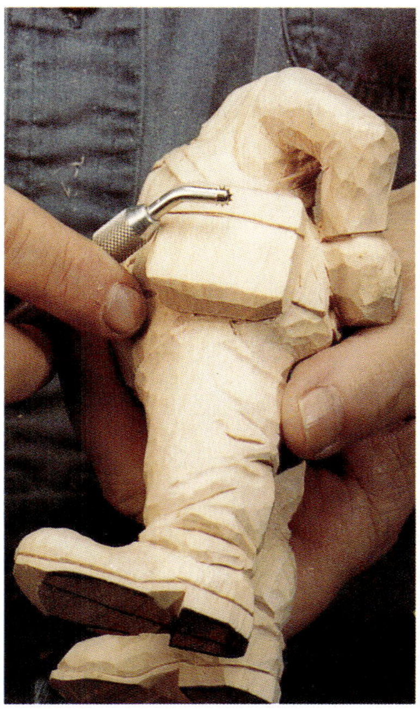

The creel needs a wicker texture, and I'm going to use a pouncewheel for the job. You can buy these in sets of three from most tool dealers.

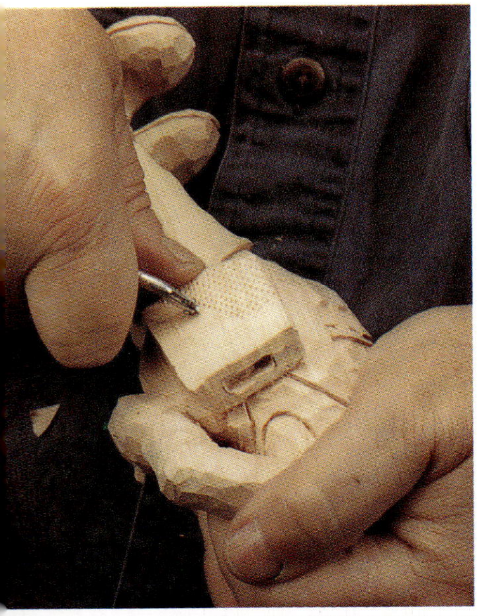

It creates a nice basket look.

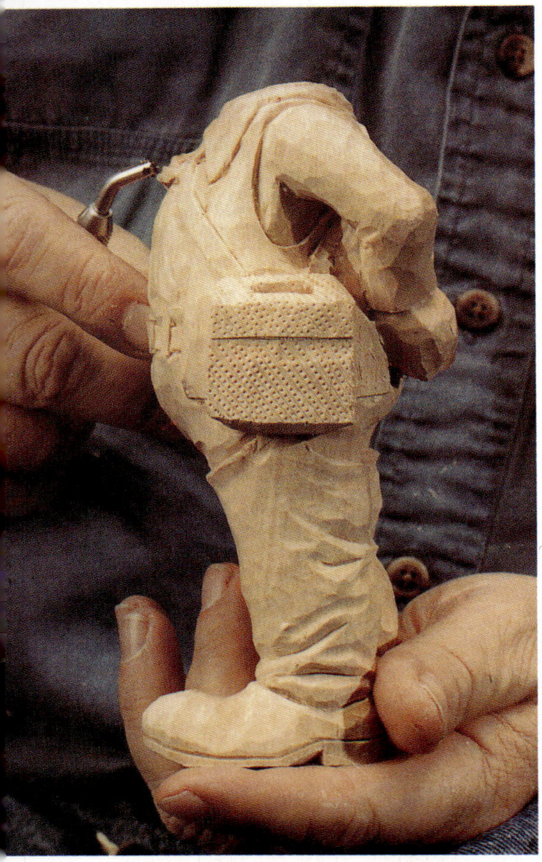

The creel.

I've put off finishing the hands until I drilled a hole in the one in front—now he can hold his fishing rod, and I can carve in more detail. It's much easier to drill the hole first. Make sure you size it correctly!

The first thing we establish is the thumb. Make a stop cut and then cut back to it from behind.

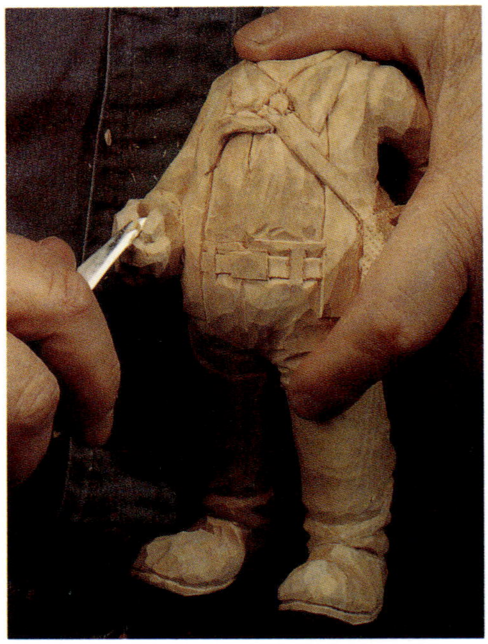

Make stop cuts all the way around the thumb—even underneath it.

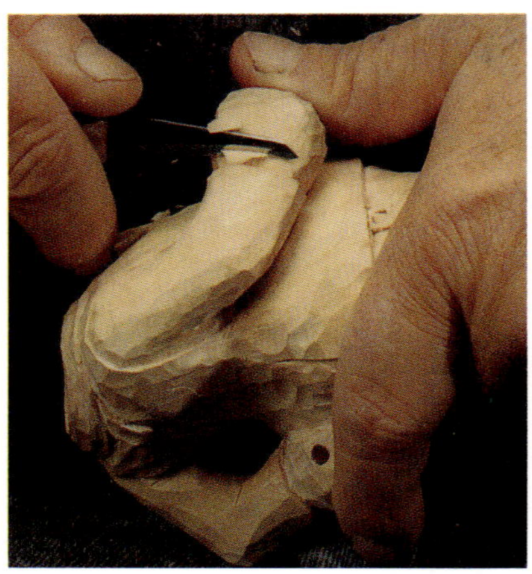

I have a system that works pretty good for the hands. Think of them in terms of four planes: The back of the hand, the knuckle to the first joint, first joint to the second, and the second to the tips. Make a flat cut away from the knuckle twards the wrist.

Remember that when the hand is making a fist, the knuckle of the thumb is in alignment with the rest of the knuckles.

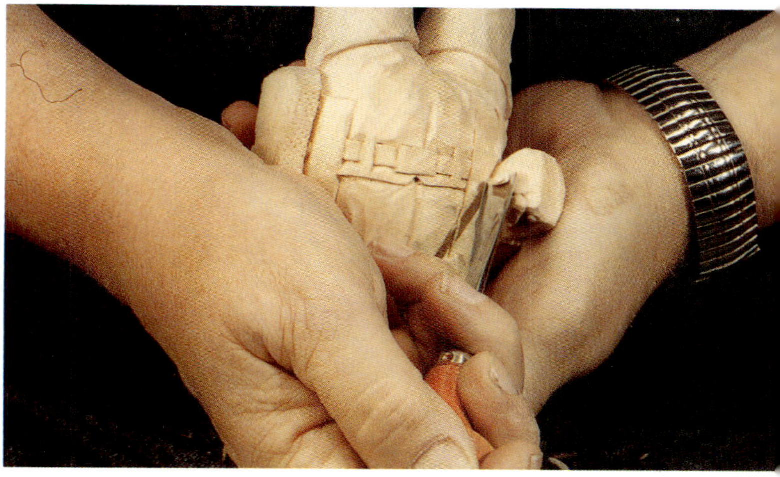

The last plane is closest to the body.

To keep the fingers in line, I let the end of the index finger disappear under the thumb. Match the joints of the thumb and finger together. It's important to make the fingers the same thickness, so check the hand underneath from time to time to make sure you're cutting evenly.

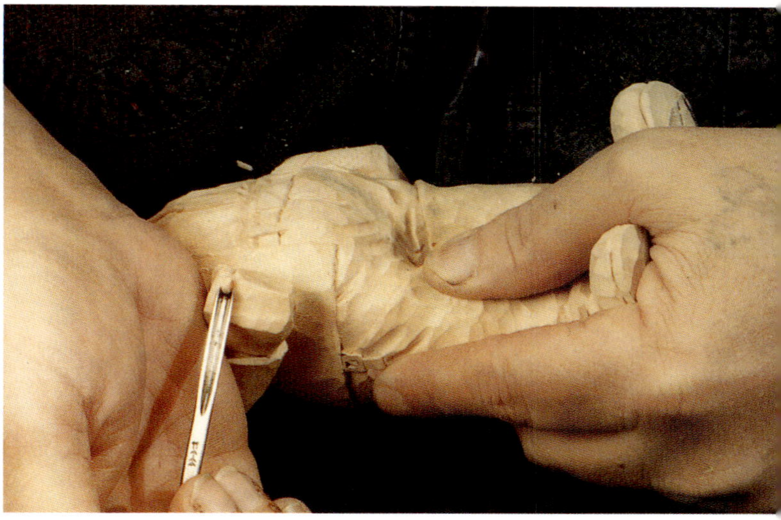

Now we can finish the fingers. I start with the index finger. I'm using a veiner. Don't cut too deep in case you need to change the proportions of the fingers.

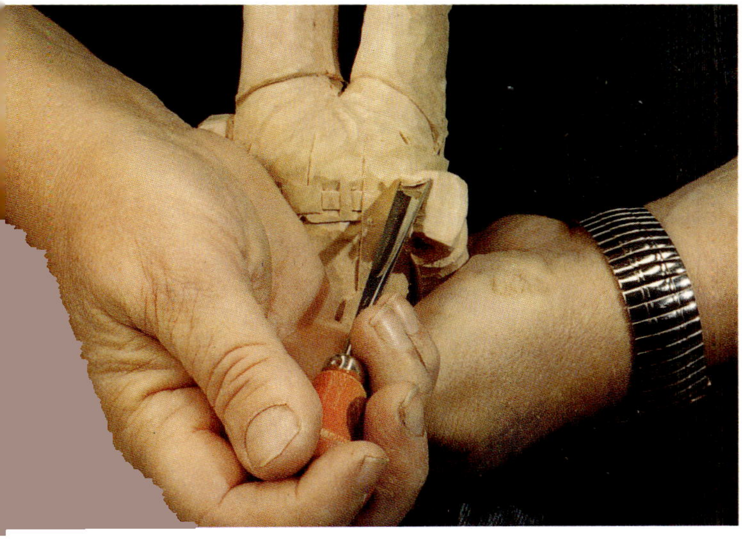

On the third plane, I'm using a flatter gouge to round the fingers out more naturally.

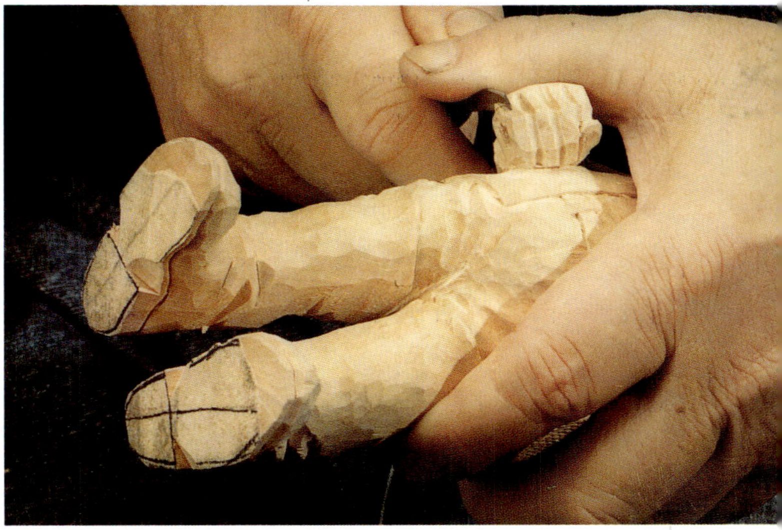

The pinky finger is too big, but instead of going back with the veiner, I'll just cut some off the end here.

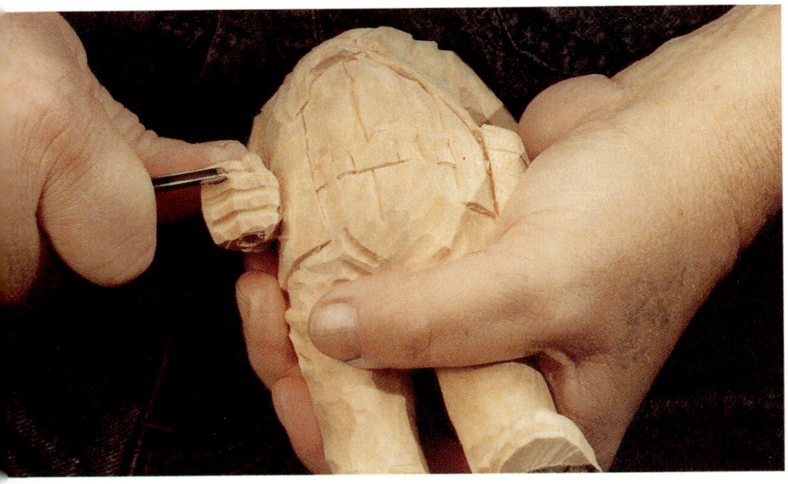

I'm using the V-tool here to go in deeper now. Don't try to go all the way around the hand in one stroke.

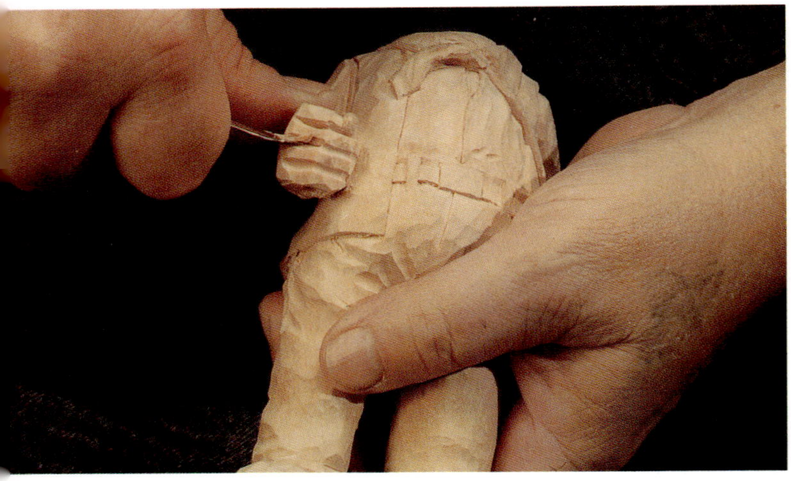

You can use a little knife like this to do the same thing in two cuts.

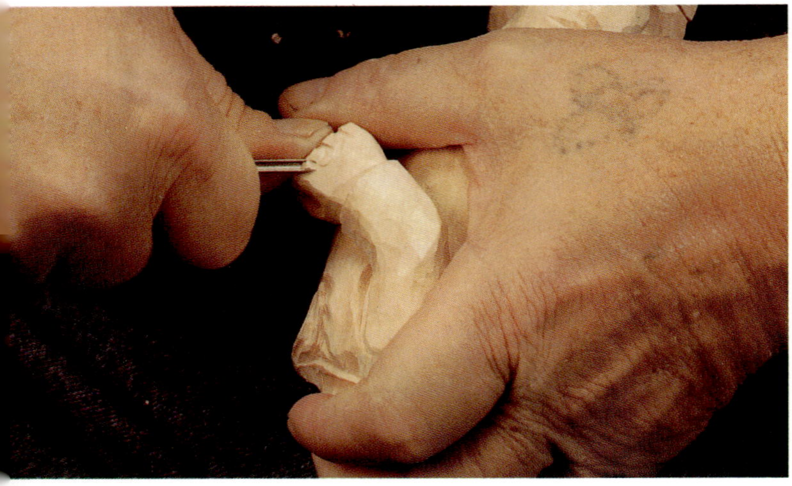

Use a half round gouge to bring out the knuckles.

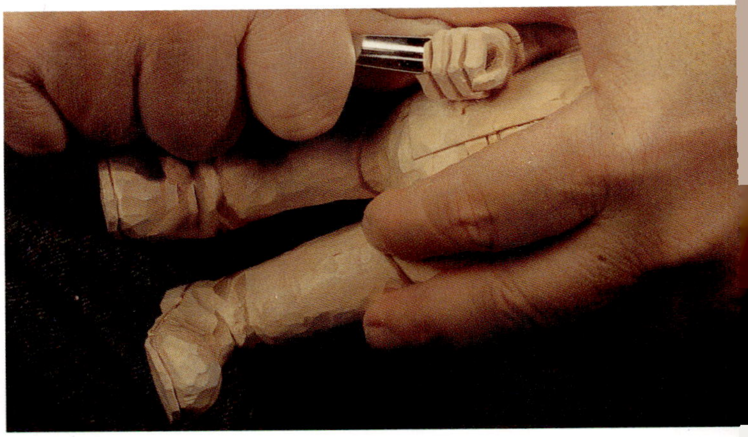

A flatter gouge brings out the other joints.

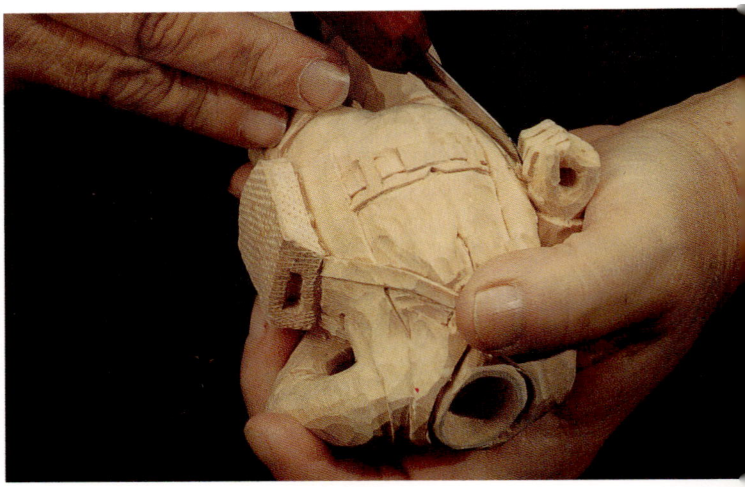

A hooked knife rounds off the finger tips.

Progress on the hand.

When you start working on the other hand, stop and think about its position. Make sure you put the thumb in the right place. We don't want two right hands!

The left hand.

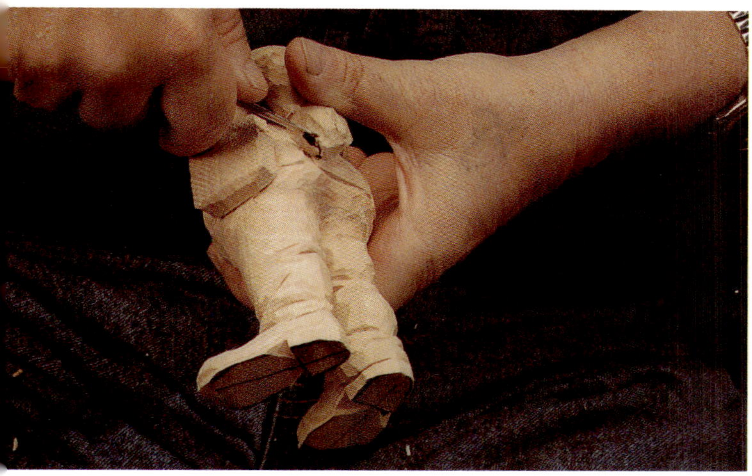

Make three deep cuts like a triangle to define the thumb. I've drilled a smaller hole for the other end of the fishing rod, but it's positioned differently.

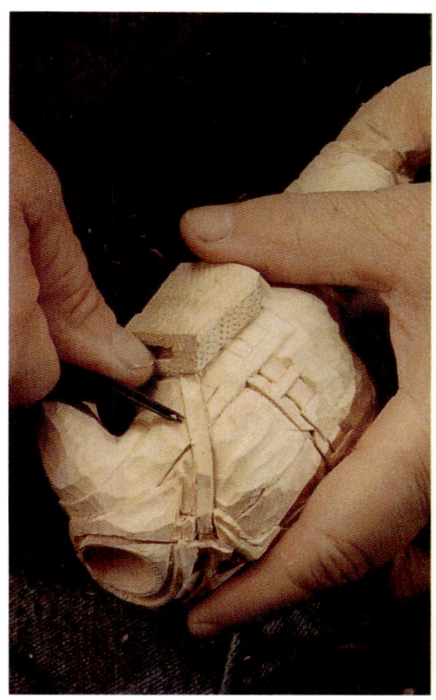

The vest needs some pockets. I did some pencil sketches and now I'm making straight cuts with the V-tool away from the pocket to make it stand out from the vest. It's important to keep the V-tool sharp.

Now we move on to making the four planes.

Pockets.

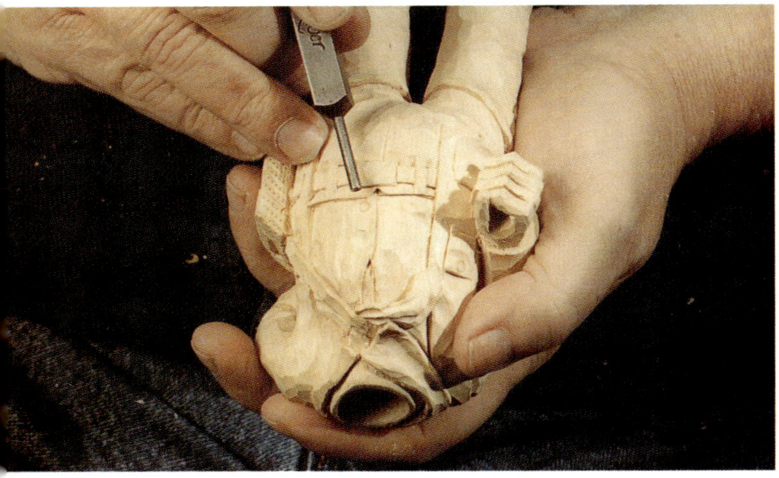

I'm using a punch for the buttons.

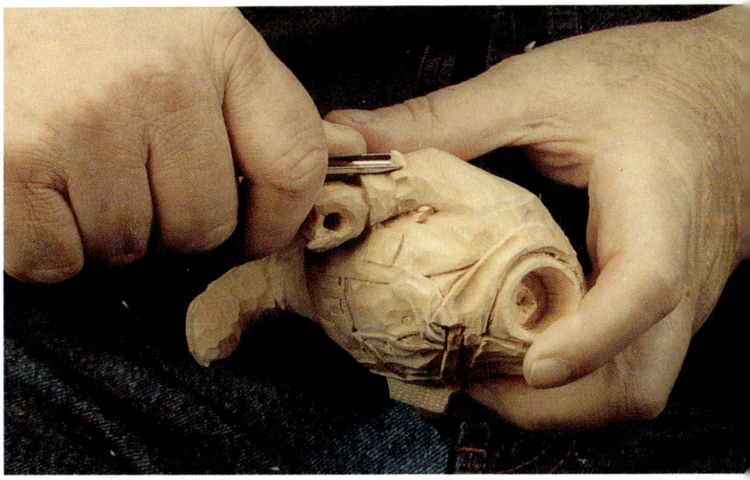

Some nips with the half round give a blousy effect.

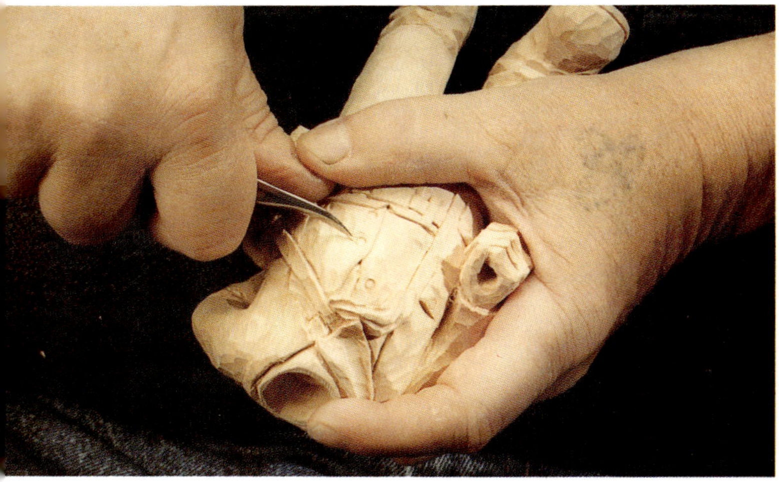

For the edge of the buttonhole to peek out, I make two small cuts at the far edge of the button.

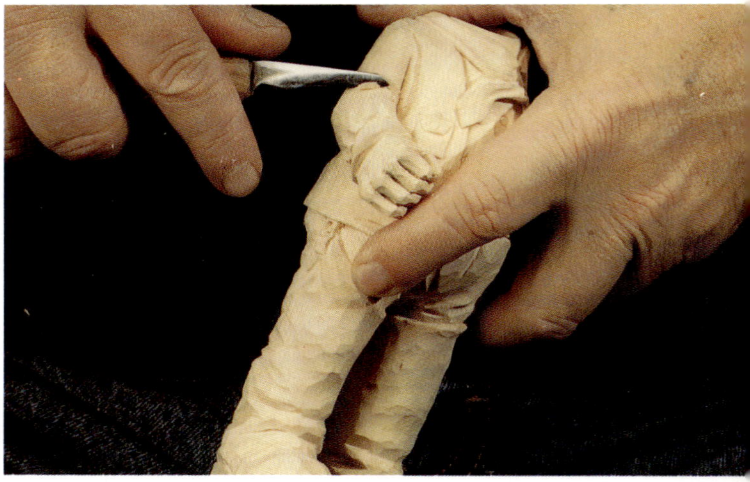

Make a crow's foot shaped wrinkle in the crook of the arm.

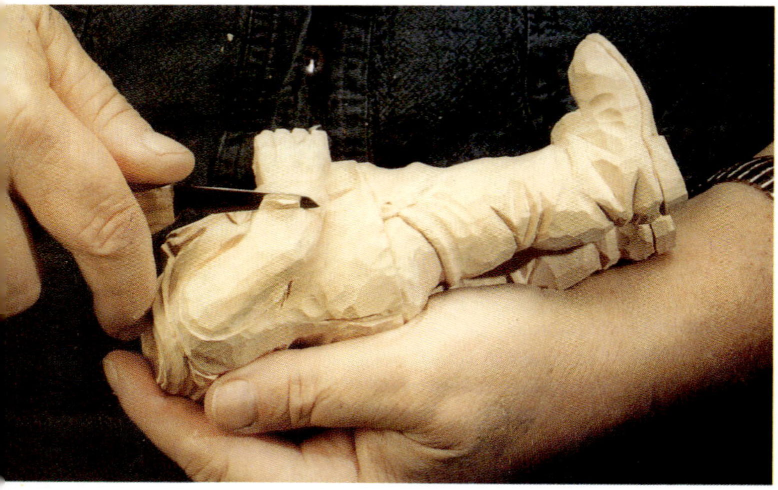

For the cuffs, I made a stop cut and I'm working back to it from the end of the sleeve.

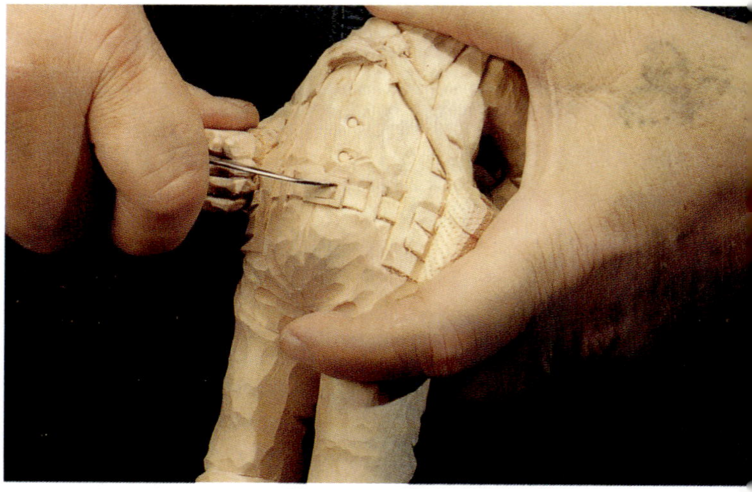

For the belt buckle, start by poking out the corners with the knife.

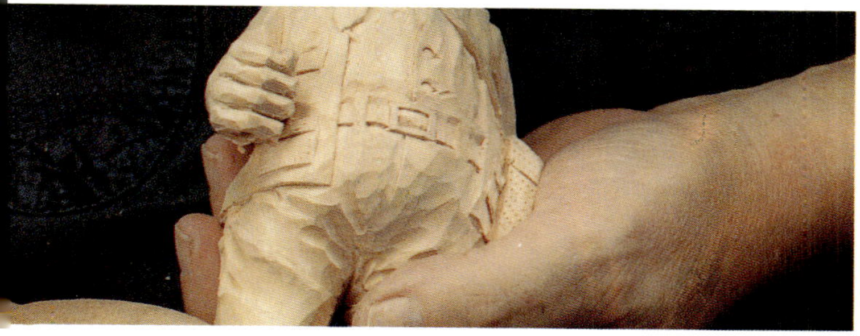

Dig out cuts between each corner.

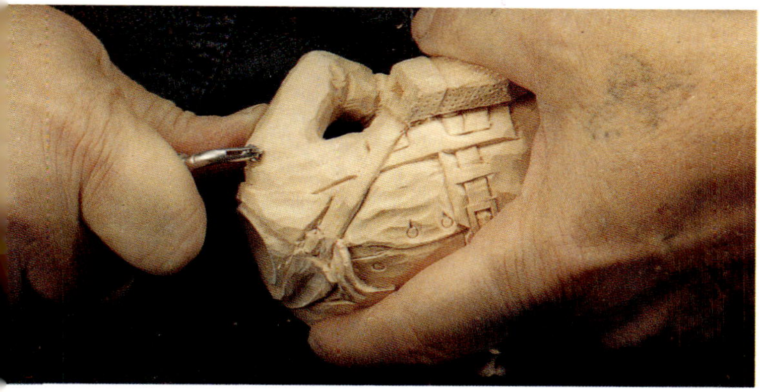

We'll go back to the pounce wheel to finish the clothes, giving them a nice seam effect. Paint really brings it out.

I've decided that our fisherman needs a fish for his creel. I'm drawing a pattern first.

I laid the pattern on a piece of wood and cut it out with the band saw. I left a little stick on it with the grain so I'll have something to hold on to.

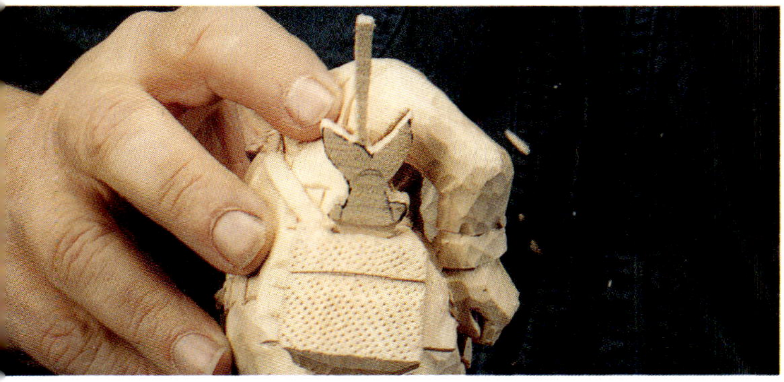

I left enough at the other end to have a little tab to fit in the hole in the creel. You may have to cut it down some to make it fit.

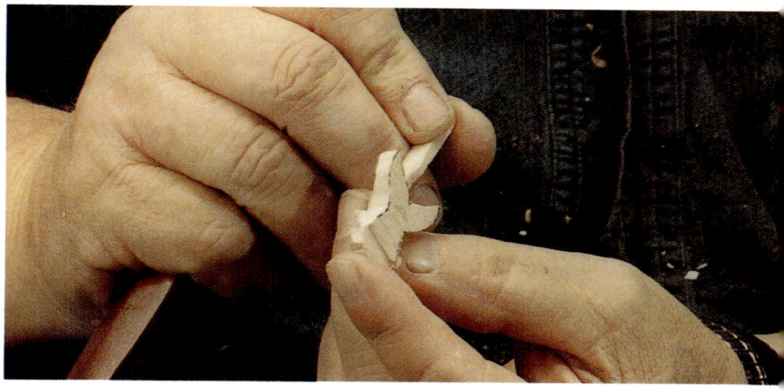

I'm starting with the fins. I'm making them curl a little bit to make it look like the fish is flopping around.

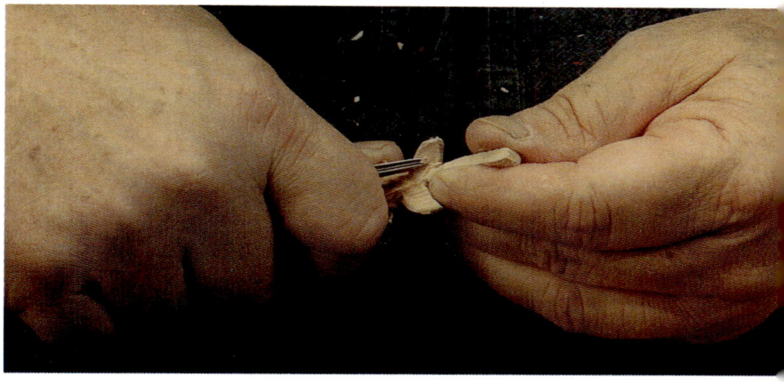

The tail needs to curve around too, and I'm using a veiner to give it some texture.

The fish tail. I've left that little stick on there to hold on to when I paint it.

Progress. Now we're ready to paint!

Painting the Project

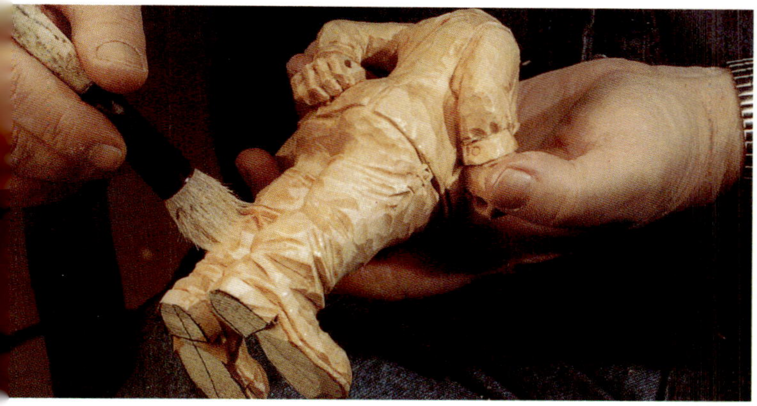

First, I paint on an undercoat of boiled linseed oil. It really brings out the color in the oil paint we're about to use.

The same applies for the base of the neck. I like to start with the flesh colors first. My basic flesh color is two parts white, one part "flesh" color (right out of the tube), and one part raw sienna. I have thinned the paints with turpentine.

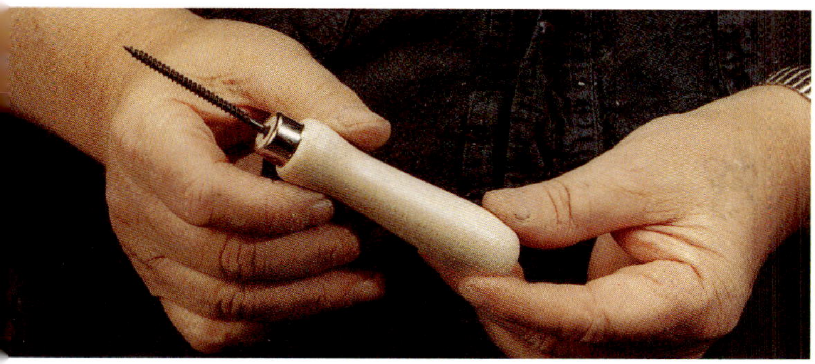

I am going to show you how to make a neat tool for the painting process. Use a file handle from any hardware or craft store, and press in a screw, anywhere from 1 1/4 to 2 inches. Glue it in with epoxy and give it time to dry.

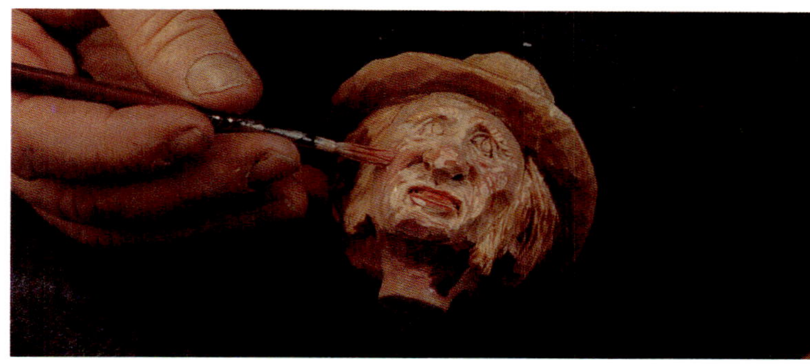

Now blend in some red for the cheeks and lips. Do the hands the same way.

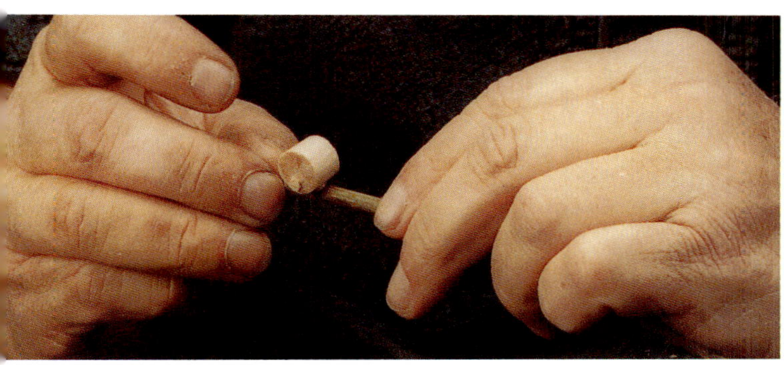

I picked a young, flexible twig from a tree for the rod, and I sawed the tip from a dowel to make a reel that can be glued on. I notched the dowel slightly for a better fit.

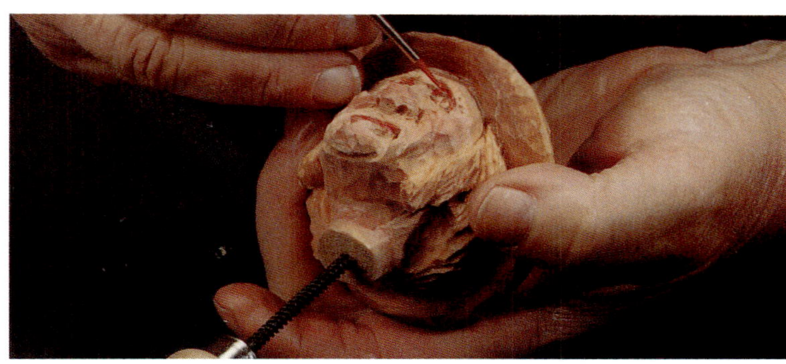

A little red over the eyes helps them stand out a little more.

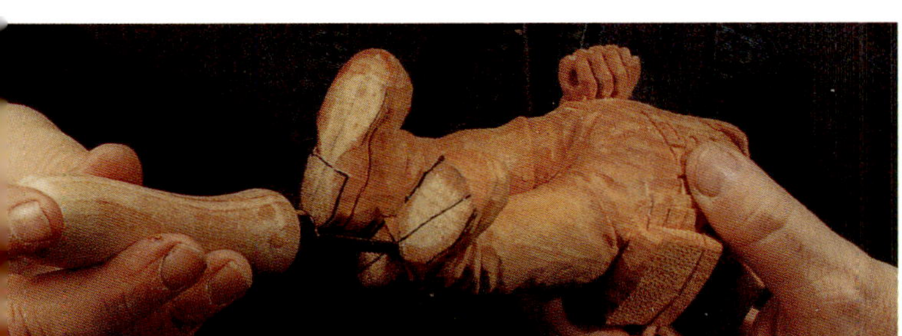

Use the tool I just made to screw into the heel slightly, where the wood is solid and strong. Don't screw it in too deep.

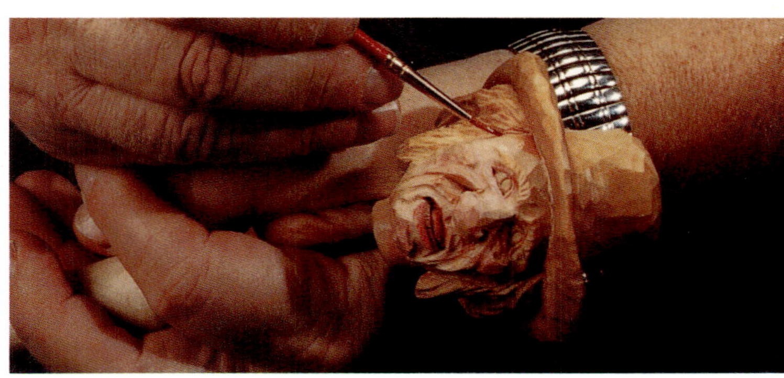

I add burnt sienna to enhance the shadows: under the chin, around the nose, and under the hat.

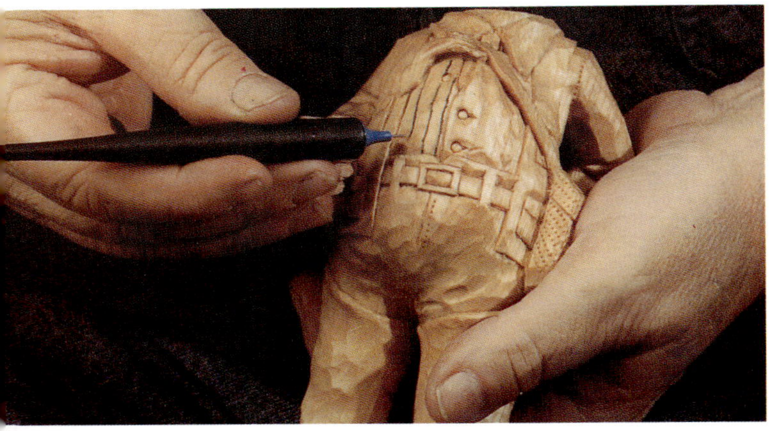

He should have a plaid shirt on, I think; I'll mark the stripes first.

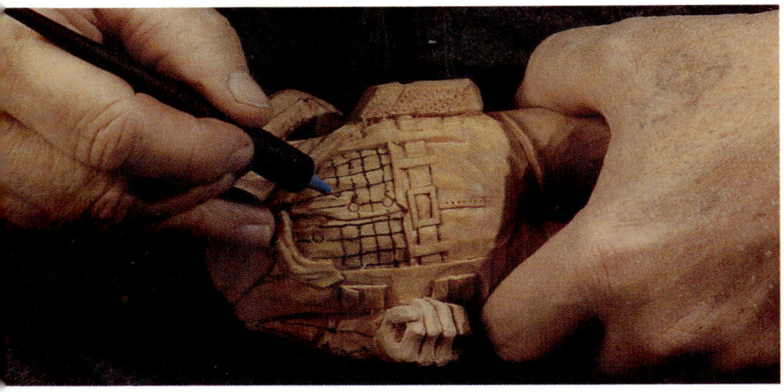

Then do the horizontal stripes. I want to be using pen here so it will show through the paint. I'm using a Grumbacher artist pen.

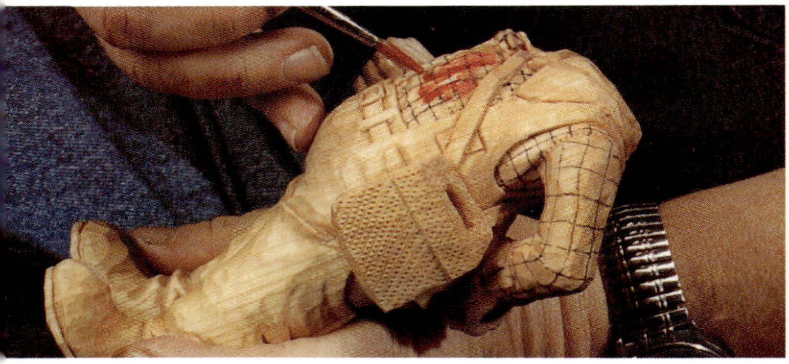

The flannel shirt will be red.

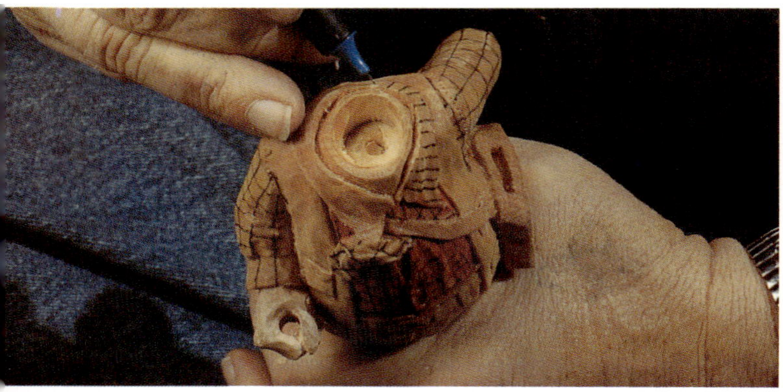

Don't forget the stripes on the collar!

Progress. The vest will stay brown. I like to leave at least one part naturally colored to show off the wood.

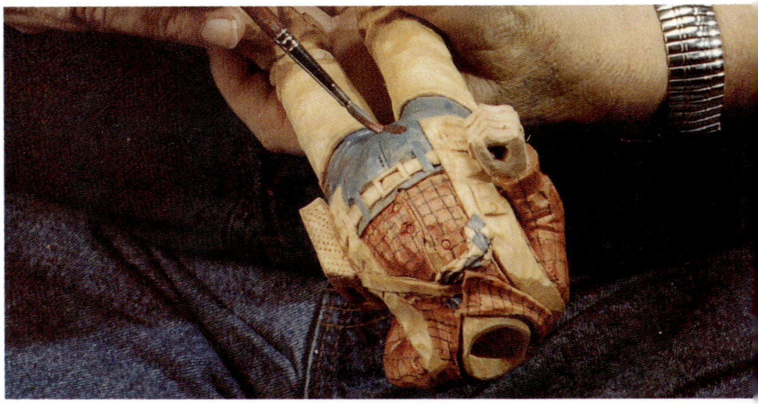

The blue jeans are next. To get a realistic look for jeans, I blend a little purple in the paint.

The hip boots will be a green that I drabbed down with some raw sienna.

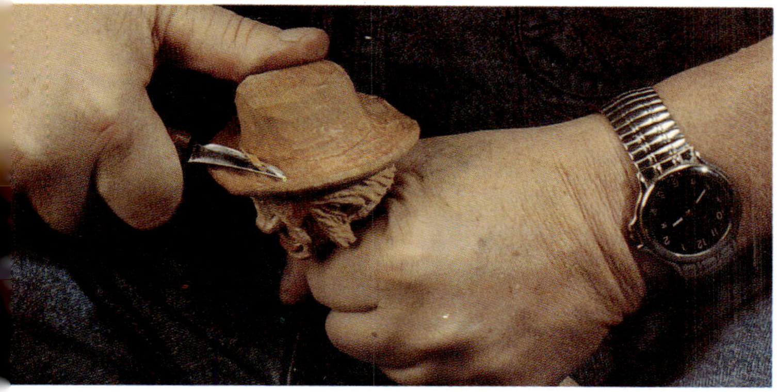

I forgot the hat band, so we'll add it real quick. Come in from the brim until the knife starts bogging down in the crown. That's a good place to put the bottom of the band.

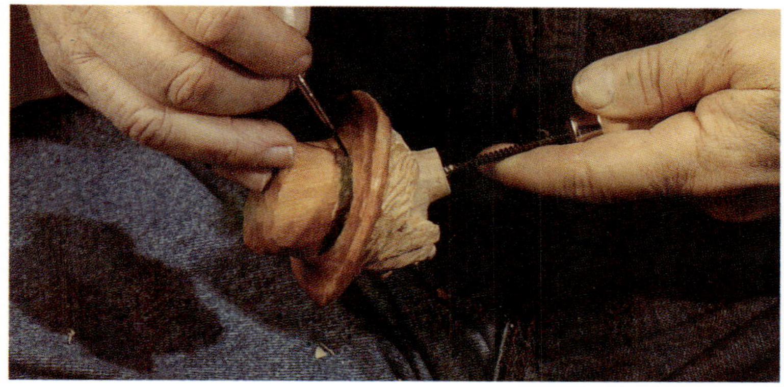

I'm using black for the band, but I'll blot most of it off with a paper towel. I'm just looking for contrast.

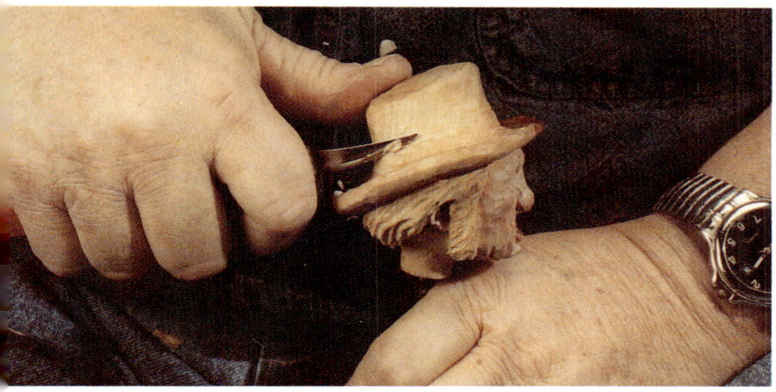

Make two straight cuts for the band, and cut towards it to raise it from the hat.

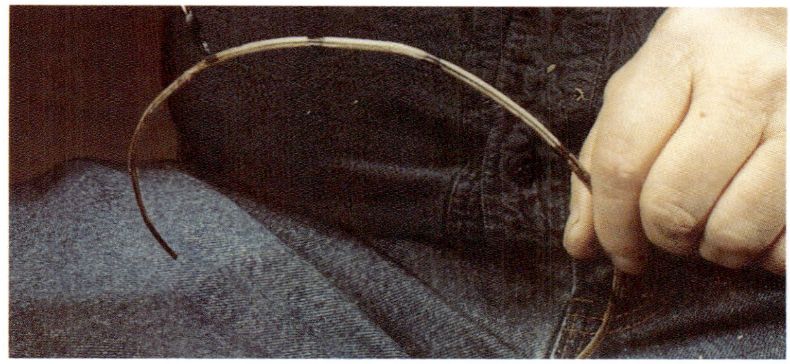

The rod and reel are ready for some paint. The handle is black, and the shaft is sienna.

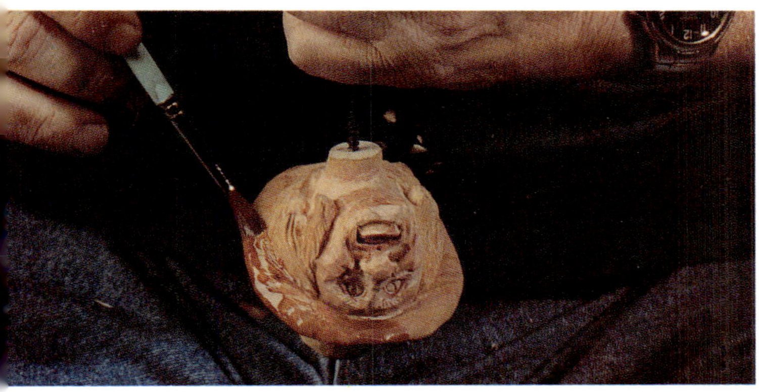

I put a coat of sienna on the underside of the brim.

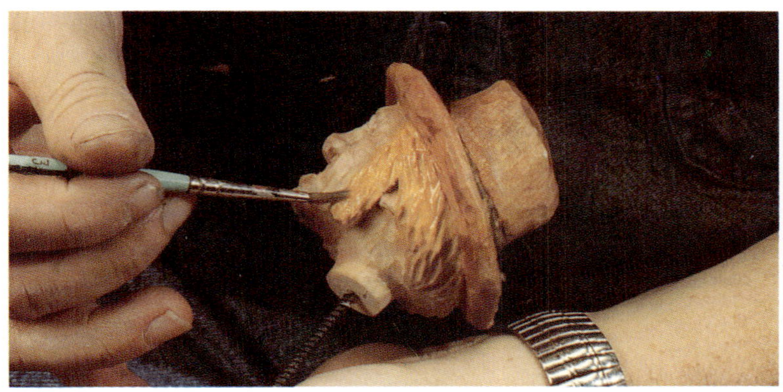

The hair is next. I'm going to try yellow; the linseed underneath should give a good color.

Progress on the head.

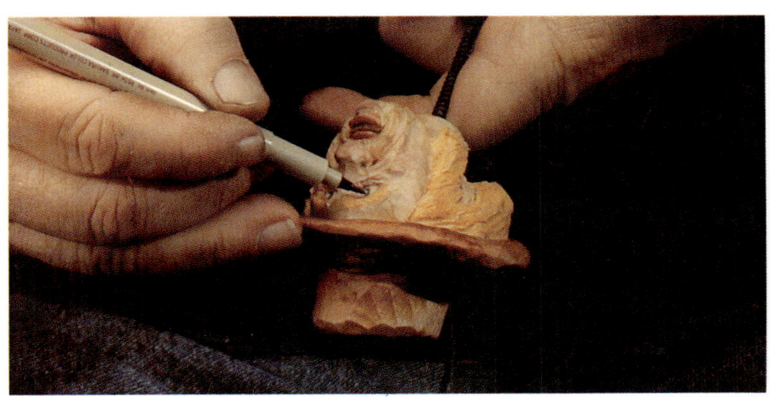

To get precision in the eye, I use a blue brush pen.

I use some lighter blue paint to fill in the rest of the iris.

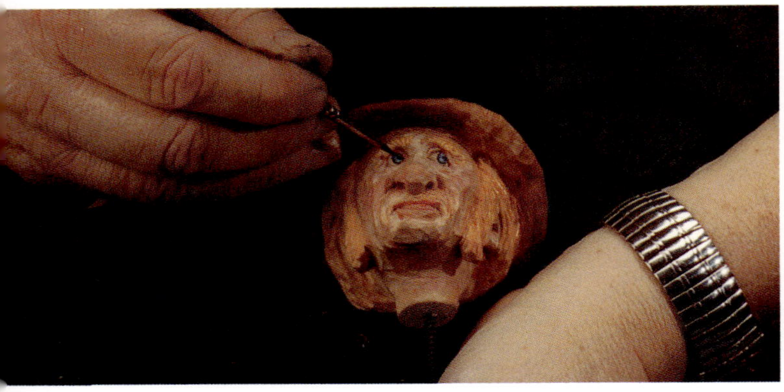

Just a touch of black for the pupil.

Finally, a speck of white for the glint in his eye and also for the teeth.

The painted head.

Some finishing details on the body: the white t-shirt collar, the buttons, the tie.

The fish should be white to start with, and then I'll work in some red and some blue. After that, I'll dot him with black pen for a more natural look.

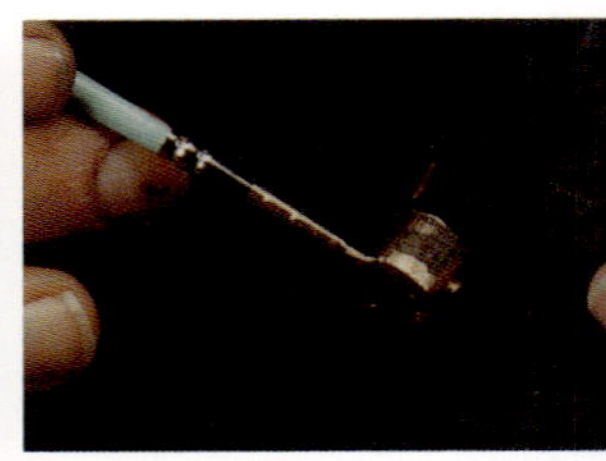

This gold leaf paint is great for touch ups on the reel...

...the buttons, and the belt buckle.

I glued the head on, the rod in the hands, and the fish into the top of the creel with a little bit of wood glue. Don't go overboard with the glue in case you want to change anything later on.

The finished figure.

I used a little sliver of wood with some red and white paint for the fly, our crowning jewel.

Featured Carving

Gallery

Outa Oder

Outa Oder

TOM WOLFE
97 ©

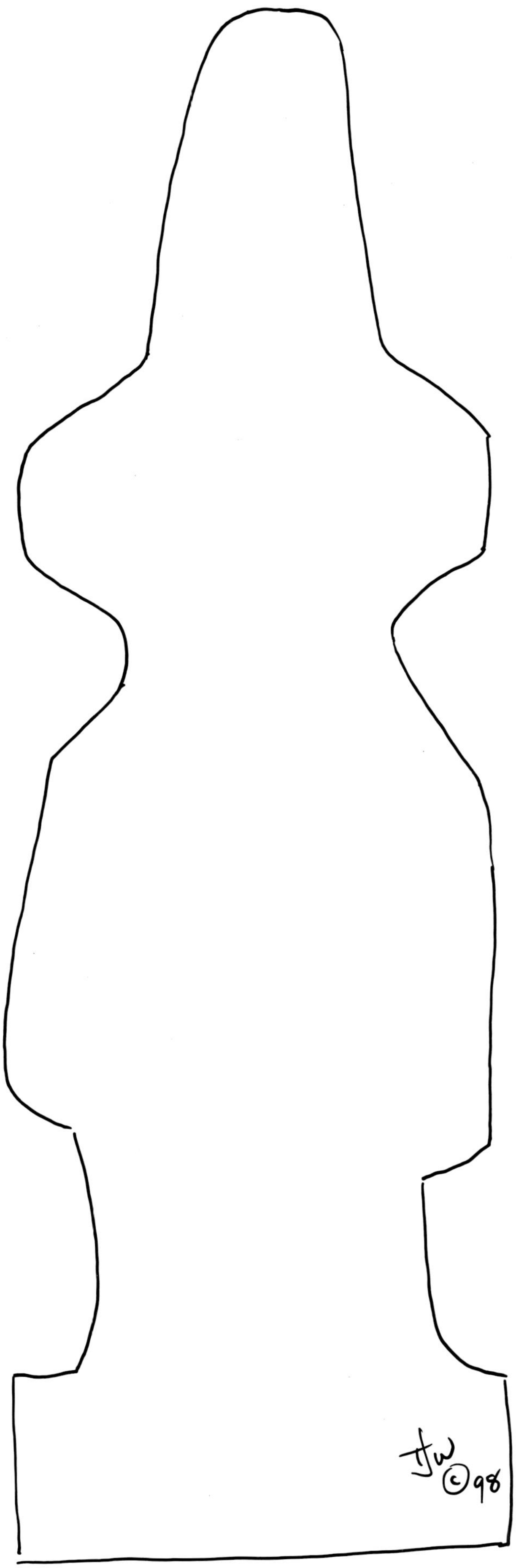
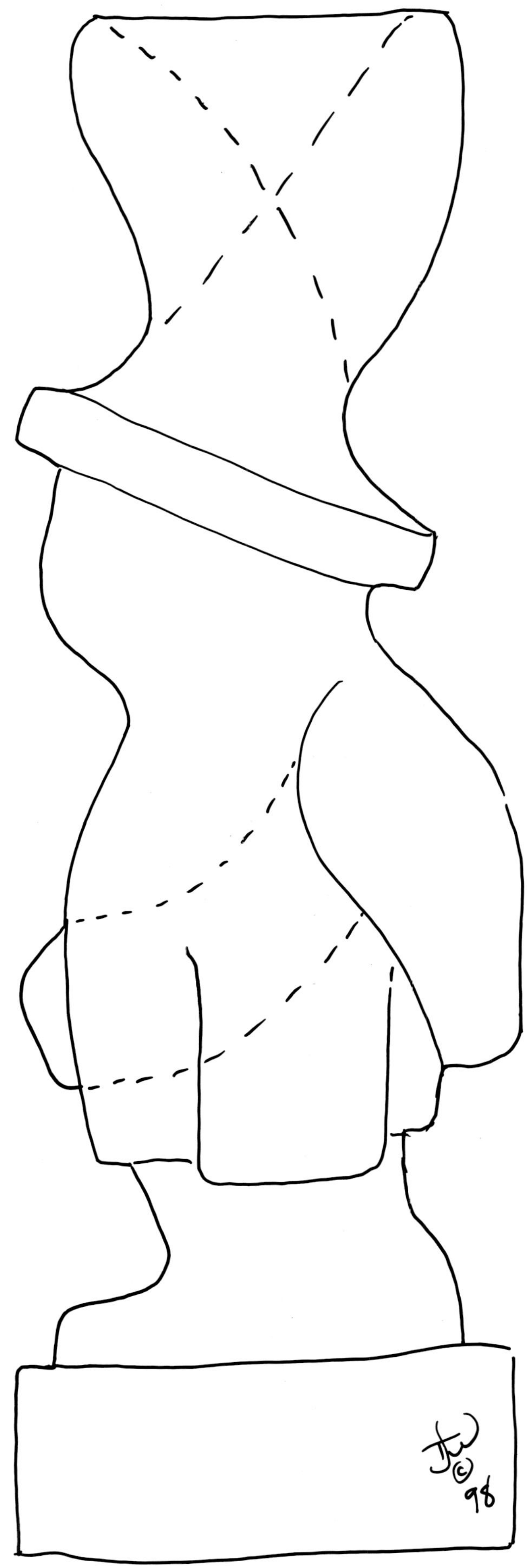